MW00950936

THE

VANITY

OF

THOUGHTS

DISCOVERED:

WITH THEIR DANGER AND CURE.

BY

THOMAS GOODWIN, B.D.

LONDON:

Reprinted at the cost and charges of the Editor, and are to be sold by

WILLIAM PAMPLIN, 45, FRITH STREET,

SOHO SQUARE.

M.D.CCCL.

T. Pettitt, Printer, 1, Old Compton Street, Soho.

TO THE READER.

~~~~~~~~~~~~~~~~~~~~~~~~~

THE subject matter of this little Book is Thoughts,—that is a good petition in the Common Prayer Book—(and indeed there are many good petitions in it)—" cleanse the Thoughts of our hearts by the inspiration of Thy Holy Spirit, &c." yet Heartwork is but little known, set by, or contended for, now-a-day by the admirers of our Common Prayer Book, but as " ARCHBISHOP" BUNYAN says, —all those whose Religion is destitute of a work of Grace in the Heart are sure to come to nothing,—he compares it to the waning moon—and God the Holy Ghost speaking by the mouth of Zophar in the Book of Job, (chap. xx. v. 6, 8,) draws a comparison which should engage the attention of every empty professor ;—O that such were wise and would lay the passage to heart,—pray turn to it and read it:—but to return to the subject of the present little treatise, THOUGHTS; it is true these do not come within the province of man's judgment, and in *that* sense, the commonly received saying "thoughts are free"—is not to be quarrelled with.—All the time that an unrenewed sinner, whether he be an openly profane ungodly one, or an outside professor, (Evangelical or otherwise, both alike vain) is a stranger to the effectual work of God the Holy Ghost in his heart, he must be classed among those fools who make a mock at sin,—but as soon as the operation of the Spirit quickens the poor dead sinner, feeling arises out of insensibility and life is found where death only reigned before;—and this may be seen clear enough in every example left upon record in the Word of God—two instances occur to the mind,—Saul the persecutor, and the nameless Jailer,—the first crys out " Lord what wouldst thou have me to do"? the other, "what must I do to be saved"?—very similar language you see, and the Apostle Paul lets us a little into what took place behind the scenes in his case, says he, " I was alive without the Law once,"—as whole hearted and as insensible and unfeeling as any proud Pharisee, or lifeless Antinomian in the world—but when once the holy, just, and good Law was applied with a little of that power with which it will one day be invested, to condemn and to confound the sinner whom now it fails to convince,— " when the commandment came," says Paul, " sin revived and I died:" just so has it been felt in the experience of saved sinners in all ages; conviction of sin must of necessity form the groundwork of all real vital Godliness; where this has once passed upon the sinner he can cordially fall in with, and own, this for a truth—" the Thought of foolishness is sin," because God, having set his secret sins in the light of His countenance, has shewn him, how that He is acquainted with, and takes notice of, all the actings and outgoings of his thoughts and affections; and He causes the earnest desire of the poor creature's heart to be this; Oh when shall it once be, that every thought may be captivated, or brought into sweet captivity to the obedience of Christ? and sooner or later God is pleased to give testimony in that sinner's conscience to His own word, that "the Thoughts of the justified man are right."

Reader, do you know anything of this kind of Religion? if you do, this little book is likely enough to suit you: before we part allow a word of admonition and advice;

First, cultivate a holy familiarity at a Throne of Grace, and a growing acquaintance with the written Word of God; there is a soul satisfying sweetness in Communion with God which no words can describe, "acquaint now thyself with Him and be at peace," or in New Testament language, "the peace of God which passeth all understanding shall keep your heart and mind through Christ Jesus."

Second, let me add, shun the companionship of fools and such as are wise in their own conceits; take heed of Professors, the general run of (so called) evangelical Professors, do not be hasty in making religious acquaintances, but seek rather the society of those who can relate something of what God has done for their souls, who can speak of the glory of His Kingdom, and talk of His power, you will soon learn to discriminate (if you look up simply for divine guidance) between, what may not improperly be called Exeter Hall Professors, as light as vanity can make them, and the sincere simple hearted followers of the Lord Jesus Christ.

That you may profit by reading is the prayer of

The EDITOR.

WALTHAM ABBEY,
　September 26, 1849.

*** It appears from the worthy Author's own account of this little work, compared with his Son's Biographical Sketch of the good man, (prefixed to the fifth volume of his whole works)—that it formed the substance of certain Sermons preached to the Town of Cambridge, at Trinity Church there, in the year 1629.—The earliest edition (so far as I am aware of) of the " Vanity of Thoughts," is that printed in small 18mo. in the year 1637, it was again printed in the same small size in 1638—in small 4to. also, in the same year,—reprinted in the small 4to. collection of his minor works, in two volumes, 1650, and in the third of the five folio volumes in 1692, published after his death, by his Son; the present reprint is from the first, (1637) carefully collated with all the subsequent editions.

CONTENTS.

A TABLE

Of those Scriptures upon which some light is cast in this Treatise.

THE

VANITY of THOUGHTS.

How long shall thy vain thoughts lodge within thee?—Jeremiah iv. 14.

IN these words he compares the heart unto some house of common resort, made as it were with many and large rooms to entertain and lodge multitudes of Guests in; into which, before conversion, all the vain, light, wanton, profane, dissolute thoughts, that post up and down the World (as your thoughts do) and run riot all the day, have free, open access, the heart keeps open house to them, gives them willing, cheerful welcome, and entertainment; accompanies them, travels o'er all the world for the daintiest pleasures to feed them with ; *Lodgeth,* harbours them, and there they, like unruly gallants and rioters, *lodge,* and revel it day and night, and defile those rooms they lodge in, with their loathsome filth and vomits. *How long,* says the Lord, *shall they lodge therein? Whilst I* with my Spirit, my Son, and train of graces, *stand at the door and knock, Rev.* iii. 20. and cannot find admittance ; from all which filthiness, &c. the *Heart,* this house, must be *washed ; wash thy heart from wickedness* : *washed,* not swept only of grosser evils (as *Matth.* xii. 43. the *house, the unclean spirit re-enters into* is said to be swept of evils that lay loose and uppermost) but *washed,* and cleansed of those defilements which stick more close, and are incorporated, and in-wrought into the spirit. And 2. those *vain* and unruly guests must be turned out of doors, without any warning, they have staid there long enough ; too long ; *How long?* says our prophet here, and the *time past may suffice,* as the Apostle speaks,

Jer. 4:14 O Jerusalem, wash thine heart from wickedness, that thou mayest be saved. How long shall thy vain thoughts lodge within thee?

Rev. 3:20 Behold, I stand at the door, and knock: if any man hear my voice, and open the door, I will come in to him, and will sup with him, and he with me.

Matt. 12:43-45 When the unclean spirit is gone out of a man, he walketh through dry places, seeking rest, and findeth none. Then he saith, I will return into my house from whence I came out; and when he is come, he findeth it empty, swept, and garnished. Then goeth he, and taketh with himself seven other spirits more wicked than himself, and they enter in and dwell there: and the last state of that man is worse than the first. Even so shall it be also unto this wicked generation.

they must lodge there no more. The house, the soul, is not in conversion to be pulled down, but only these guests turned out; and though kept out they cannot be, they will still enter whilst we are in these houses of clay, yet lodge they must not: if thoughts of anger and revenge come in, in the morning or day time, they must be turned out e're night, *Let not the Sun go down upon your wrath, Ephes.* iv. 26. for so you may come to lodge yet a worse guest in your heart with them: *Give not place to the Devil,* (so it follows) who will *bring seven worse with him.* If unclean thoughts offer to come to bed to thee, when thou liest down, let them not lodge with thee. To conclude, it is not what thoughts are in your hearts, and pass through them, as what lodging they have, that doth difference your repentance: many good thoughts and motions may pass, as *Strangers* through a bad man's heart; and so likewise multitudes of vain thoughts may make a thoroughfare of a believer's heart, and disturb him in good duties, by knockings and inter-

Eph. 4:26-27 Be ye angry, and sin not: let not the sun go down upon your wrath: Neither give place to the devil.

ruptions, and breakings in upon the heart of a good man; but still they lodge not there; are not fostered, harboured.

My scope in our ordinary course is, to discover the wickedness and vanity of the heart by nature: in the heart we are yet but in the upper parts of it, the understanding and the defilements thereof, which are to be washed out of it; and the next defilement, which in my broken order I mean to handle, is that which is here specified, *the vanity of your thoughts:* for the discovery sake of of which only, I chose this text as my ground; *that* is it, therefore, which I will chiefly insist upon. A *subject* which, I confess, would prove of all else the vastest, so as to make an exact particular discovery of the vanities in our thoughts. To travel over the whole creation, and to take a survey and give an account of all that vanity that abounds in all the creatures, was (as you know) the task of the wisest of men, *Solomon;* the flower of his studies and labours: but the *vanities of our thoughts,* are multiplied as much in us, and more, this *little world* affords more varieties of vanities, than the great. Our thoughts made the *creatures subject to vanity, Rom.* viii. 20, therefore themselves are subject to vanity much more. In handling of them I will show you, 1. what is meant by *Thoughts.* 2. *What by vanity.* 3. *That our thoughts are vain.* 4. Wherein that vanity doth consist, both in the general, and some particulars.

First, what is *meant by thoughts,* especially as they are the intended subject of this discourse, which in so vast an argument I must necessarily set limits unto: 1. by *thoughts,* the Scriptures do comprehend all the *internal* acts of the mind of man, of what faculty soever, all those reasonings, consultations, purposes, resolutions, intents, ends, desires, and cares of the mind of man, as opposed to our *external* words and actions, so in *Isaiah* lxvi. 18. All acts are divided into those two, *I know their works and their thoughts*: what is transacted within the mind is called the *thoughts*; what thereof do manifest

Rom 8:20 For the creature was made subject to vanity, not willingly, but by reason of him who hath subjected the same in hope

Is. 66:18 For I know their works and their thoughts: it shall come, that I will gather all nations and tongues; and they shall come, and see my glory.

themselves, and break out in actions, are called *works*. And so *Genesis* vi. 5. *Every imagination of the thoughts,* (omne figmentum) i. e. all the creatures that the mind of man frames within itself, purposes, desires, &c. (as it is noted in the margin) *are evil;* where by thoughts are understood all that *comes within the mind,* (as *Ezekiel*. xi. 5. the phrase is) and so indeed we vulgarly use it, and understand it, *to remember* a man, is, to *think of him, Genesis*. xl. 14. to have *purposed* a thing, we say, *I thought to do it;* to take *care* about a business, is to *take thought,* 1. *Samuel* ix. 5. And the reason, why all in man's heart may thus be called *the thoughts,* is, because indeed, all affections, desires, purposes, are stirred up by thoughts, bred, fomented, and nourished by them : no one thought passeth, but it stirreth some affection of fear, joy, care, grief, &c. Now, although they are thus *largely* taken here, yet I intend not to handle the *vanity* of them in so large a sense at present : I must confine myself, as strictly as may be,

Gen. 6:5 And God saw that the wickedness of man was great in the earth, and that every imagination of the thoughts of his heart was only evil continually.

Ez. 11:5 And the Spirit of the Lord fell upon me, and said unto me, Speak; Thus saith the Lord; Thus have ye said, O house of Israel: for I know the things that come into your mind, every one of them.

Gen. 40:14 But think on me when it shall be well with thee, and shew kindness, I pray thee, unto me, and make mention of me unto Pharaoh, and bring me out of this house

1 Sam. 9:5 And when they were come to the land of Zuph, Saul said to his servant that was with him, Come, and let us return; lest my father leave caring for the asses, and take thought for us.

to the vanity of that, which is more *properly* called the *thinking, meditating, considering power of man,* which is in his understanding or spirit, that being the subject I have in hand: *Thoughts* not being in this sense opposed only to *your works,* but unto purposes and intents, so *Hebrews* iv. 12. as the *soul* and *spirit,* so thoughts and intents seem to be opposed. And *Job* xx. 2, 3. *Thoughts* are appropriated to the *spirit of understanding.* And again yet more strictly, for in the understanding I mean not to speak of, generally, all thoughts therein, neither, as not of the *reasonings* or *deliberations* in our actions: but those musings only in the *speculative* part.

And so, I can no otherwise express them to you, than thus. Those same first, more *simple conceits, apprehensions* that arise; those *fancies, meditations,* which the understanding by the *help of fancy frames within itself of things;* those whereon your minds ponder and pore, and muse upon things, these I mean by *thoughts,* I mean those

Heb. 4:12 For the word of God is quick, and powerful, and sharper than any twoedged sword, piercing even to the dividing asunder of soul and spirit, and of the joints and marrow, and is a discerner of the thoughts and intents of the heart.
Job 20:2-3 Therefore do my thoughts cause me to answer, and for this I make haste. I have heard the check of my reproach, and the spirit of my understanding causeth me to answer.

_____

_____

_____

_____

_____

_____

_____

_____

_____

_____

_____

_____

_____

talkings of our minds with the things we know, as the Scripture calls it, *Proverbs* vi. 22. those same parleys, interviews, chattings, the mind hath with the things let into it, with the things we fear, with the things we love: for all these things our minds make their companions, and our thoughts hold them discourse, and have a thousand conceits about them; this I mean by *thoughts.* For besides that *reasoning* power, *deliberating* power, whereby we ask ourselves continually, *what shall we do?* and whereby we reason and discuss things, which is a more inward closet, the Cabinet and privy council of the heart, there is a more outward lodging, that presence chamber, which entertains all comers, which is the *thinking, meditating, musing* power in man, which suggesteth matter for deliberations, and consultations, and reasonings, which holds the *objects* till we view them, which entertaineth all that come to speak with any of our affections.

2. I add, which *the mind frames within itself,* so the Scripture expresseth their orig-

Prov. 6:22 When thou goest, it shall lead thee; when thou sleepest, it shall keep thee; and when thou awakest, it shall talk with thee.

inal to us, and their manner of rising, *Proverbs* vi. 14. *Frowardness is in his heart, he forgeth mischief,* (*fabricatur,*) as a Smith does Iron, hammers it out : and the thoughts are the materials of this frowardness in us; upon all the things which are presented to us, the mind begets some thoughts, imaginations on them ; and as *lusts,* *James* i. 15. so *thoughts Isaiah* lix. 4. are conceived. *They conceive mischief, and bring forth iniquity, and hatch Cockatrice eggs, and weave Spider's webs.* And *verse* vii. he instanceth in *thoughts of iniquity,* because our thoughts are spun out of our own hearts, are eggs of our own laying, though the things presented to us be from without.

And this I add to sever them from such *thoughts* as are *injected,* and cast in, only from without, which are children of anothers begetting, and often laid at our doors : such as are blasphemous thoughts cast in *by Satan,* wherein if the soul be merely passive, (as the word buffetting implies, 2. *Corin-*

Prov. 6:14 Frowardness is in his heart, he deviseth mischief continually; he soweth discord.
James 1:15 Then when lust hath conceived, it bringeth forth sin: and sin, when it is finished, bringeth forth death.
Is. 59:4-5,7 None calleth for justice, nor any pleadeth for truth: they trust in vanity, and speak lies; they conceive mischief, and bring forth iniquity. They hatch cockatrice' eggs, and weave the spider's web: he that eateth of their eggs dieth, and that which is crushed breaketh out into a viper... Their feet run to evil, and they make haste to shed innocent blood: their thoughts are thoughts of iniquity; wasting and destruction are in their paths.

_____

_____

_____

_____

_____

_____

_____

_____

_____

_____

_____

_____

thians xii. 7.) they are none of your thoughts, but his; wherein a man is but as one in a room with another, where he hears another swear and curse, but cannot get out from him; such thoughts, if they be only *from without*, defile not a man : for *nothing defiles a man, but what comes from within, Matthew* xv. 18. 19. or which the heart hath, begotten upon it by the devil, as thoughts of uncleanness, &c., wherein though he be the father, yet the heart is the mother and womb; and therefore accordingly they affect the heart, as natural children do, and by that we may distinguish them from the other, namely, when we have a soft heart, an inward love unto them, so that our hearts do kiss the child, then they are our *thoughts*, or when the heart broods upon these eggs, then they are our *thoughts*, though they come from without.

    Though this is to be added, that even those thoughts, wherein the soul is passive, and which Satan casts in, which we do no ways own, wherein he *ravisheth* the heart, rather

2 Cor. 12:7 And lest I should be exalted above measure through the abundance of the revelations, there was given to me a thorn in the flesh, the messenger of Satan to buffet me, lest I should be exalted above measure.

Matt. 15:18-19 But those things which proceed out of the mouth come forth from the heart; and they defile the man. For out of the heart proceed evil thoughts, murders, adulteries, fornications, thefts, false witness, blasphemies

than *begets* them on us, (if there be not any consent to them in us, then it is but a *rape*, as in law it is not) I yield those thoughts are punishments often of neglect of our thoughts, and of our suffering them to wander; as *Dinah,* because she went out of curiosity, *to view the daughters of the land,* was taken and ravished, though against her will: yet it was a punishment of her curiosity : or else they are the punishment of the neglect of good motions of the spirit; which resisting, *we thereby grieve him,* and so he deals with us, as we with our children, suffers us to be scared with bugbears, and to be grieved by *Satan,* that we may learn what it is to neglect him, and harbour vanity. Lastly, I add, which the mind, *in and by itself,* or by the help of fancy, thus begets and entertains, because there are no thoughts or likenesses of things at any time in our fancies, but at the same time they are in the understanding also reflected unto it: As when two Looking-glasses are placed opposite and nigh to each other, look what object

Gen. 34:1-2 And Dinah the daughter of Leah, which she bare unto Jacob, went out to see the daughters of the land. And when Shechem the son of Hamor the Hivite, prince of the country, saw her, he took her, and lay with her, and defiled her.

Notes:

_____

_____

_____

_____

_____

_____

_____

_____

_____

_____

_____

_____

_____

appears in the one, does also in the other.

Secondly, let us see what *vanity* is, take it in all the acceptations of it; it is true of our *thoughts* that they are *vain*.

1. It is taken for *unprofitableness*. So *Ecclesiastes* i. 2. 3. *All is vanity*, because there is no profit *in them under the Sun*, such are our thoughts by nature, the wisest of them will not stand us in any stead in time of need, in time of temptation, distress of conscience, day of death or Judgement, 1. *Corinthians* 2. 6. *All the wisdom of* the wise comes to *nought. Proverbs* x. 20. *The heart of the wicked is little worth,* not a penny for them all, whereas the thoughts of a godly man are his *treasure* : *Out of the good treasure of his heart, he brings them forth.* He mints them, and they are laid up as his riches. *Psalm* cxxxix. 17. *How precious are they!* he there speaks of our *thoughts of God*, as the object of them, *thy thoughts*, that is, (*of Thee*) *are precious.*

2. *Vanity* is taken for lightness. *Lighter*

Ecc. 1:2-3 Vanity of vanities, saith the Preacher, vanity of vanities; all is vanity. What profit hath a man of all his labour which he taketh under the sun?

1 Cor. 2:6 Howbeit we speak wisdom among them that are perfect: yet not the wisdom of this world, nor of the princes of this world, that come to nought

Prov. 10:20 The tongue of the just is as choice silver: the heart of the wicked is little worth.

Lk. 6:45 A good man out of the good treasure of his heart bringeth forth that which is good; and an evil man out of the evil treasure of his heart bringeth forth that which is evil: for of the abundance of the heart his mouth speaketh.

Ps. 139:17 How precious also are thy thoughts unto me, O God! how great is the sum of them!

than vanity is a phrase used, *Psalm* lxii. 9. and whom is it spoken of? *of men,* and if any thing in them be lighter than other, it is their *thoughts* which swim in the uppermost parts, float at the top, and are as the scum of the heart; when all the best and wisest, and deepest, and solidest *thoughts* in *Belshazzar* a Prince, were *weighed,* they were *found too light, Daniel* v. 27.

3. *Vanity* is put for *folly.* So *Proverbs* xii. 11. *vain men,* is made all one with men *void of understanding.* Such are our thoughts among other evils which are said to come *out of the heart, Mark* vii. 22. ἀφροσύνη is reckoned as one, *foolishness,* that is, thoughts that are such as *mad men* have, and fools, nothing to the purpose, of which there can be made no use, which a man knows not whence they should come, nor whither they would, *without dependance.*

4. It is put for *Inconstancy,* and *frailty,* therefore *vanity* and a *shadow* are made *synonyms, Psalm* cxliv. 4. such are our *thoughts,* flitting and perishing, as bubbles.

Ps. 62:9 Surely men of low degree are vanity, and men of high degree are a lie: to be laid in the balance, they are altogether lighter than vanity.
Dan. 5:27 TEKEL; Thou art weighed in the balances, and art found wanting.
Prov. 12:11 He that tilleth his land shall be satisfied with bread: but he that followeth vain persons is void of understanding.
Mk. 7:22 Thefts, covetousness, wickedness, deceit, lasciviousness, an evil eye, blasphemy, pride, foolishness
Ps. 144:4 Man is like to vanity: his days are as a shadow that passeth away.

―――――――

―――――――

―――――――

―――――――

―――――――

―――――――

―――――――

―――――――

―――――――

―――――――

―――――――

―――――――

―――――――

Psalm cxlvi. 4. *All their thoughts perish.*

Lastly, they are *vain*, that is, indeed, *wicked* and *sinful*; *vanity* in the text here, is yoked with *wickedness*: and *vain men*, and *sons of Belial* are all one, 2 *Chronicles* xiii. 7. And such are our thoughts by nature. *Proverbs* xxiv. 9. *The thought of foolishness is sin.* And therefore a man is to be humbled for *a proud thought, Proverbs.* xxx. 32, for so *laying hand* on the mouth is taken, as *Job* xl. 4. for being *vile in a man's own eyes.*

And because this is the sense I chiefly must insist on, in handling the *vanity of the thoughts,* and also men usually think that *thoughts are free*; I will therefore prove this to you, which is the only doctrine raised, that *Thoughts are sins.*

1. The *Law judgeth* them, *Hebrews* iv. 12. *rebukes a man* for them, 1 *Corinthians* xiv. 25. and therefore they are transgressions of the law: and so also did Christ rebuke the Pharisees for *their ill thoughts, Matthew* ix. 4. which argues the spiritual excellency of the Law, that reacheth thoughts.

Ps. 146:4 His breath goeth forth, he returneth to his earth; in that very day his thoughts perish.

2 Ch. 13:7 And there are gathered unto him vain men, the children of Belial, and have strengthened themselves against Rehoboam the son of Solomon, when Rehoboam was young and tenderhearted, and could not withstand them.

Pr. 24:9 The thought of foolishness is sin: and the scorner is an abomination to men.

Pr. 30:32 If thou hast done foolishly in lifting up thyself, or if thou hast thought evil, lay thine hand upon thy mouth.

Job 40:4 Behold, I am vile; what shall I answer thee? I will lay mine hand upon my mouth.

Heb. 4:12 For the word of God is quick, and powerful, and sharper than any twoedged sword, piercing even to the dividing asunder of soul and spirit, and of the joints and marrow, and is a discerner of the thoughts and intents of the heart.

1 Cor. 14:25 And thus the secrets of his heart are revealed; and so, falling down on his face, he will worship God and report that God is truly among you.

Mt. 9:4 And Jesus knowing their thoughts said, Wherefore think ye evil in your hearts?

2. Because they are *capable of pardon*, and must be pardoned, or we cannot be saved, *Acts* viii. 22. which argues the multitudes of *God's compassions*, seeing thoughts are so infinite.

3. They are to be *repented of*, yea repentance is expressed, as to begin at them. So *Isaiah* lv. 7. *Let the unrighteous man forsake his thoughts*; and a man is never truly and throughly wrought on, (as 2 *Corinthians* x. 4. 5.) *till every thought be brought into obedience;* which argues that they are naturally rebellious, and contrary to grace. And this also argueth the *power of grace*, which is able to *rule*, and to subdue so great an Army as our thoughts are, and command them all, as one day it will do, when we are perfectly holy.

4. *They defile the man :* and nothing defiles but sin, *Matthew* xv. 15. 16. 17. *Out of the heart proceed evil thoughts, these defile the man.*

5. They are an *abomination to the Lord*, who hates nothing but sin, and *whose pure*

Act. 8:22 Repent therefore of this thy wickedness, and pray God, if perhaps the thought of thine heart may be forgiven thee.
Is. 55:7 Let the wicked forsake his way, and the unrighteous man his thoughts: and let him return unto the LORD, and he will have mercy upon him; and to our God, for he will abundantly pardon.
2 Cor. 10:4-5 (For the weapons of our warfare are not carnal, but mighty through God to the pulling down of strong holds;) Casting down imaginations, and every high thing that exalteth itself against the knowledge of God, and bringing into captivity every thought to the obedience of Christ
Mt. 15:15-18 Then answered Peter and said unto him, Declare unto us this parable. And Jesus said, Are ye also yet without understanding? Do not ye yet understand, that whatsoever entereth in at the mouth goeth into the belly, and is cast out into the draught? But those things which proceed out of the mouth come forth from the heart; and they defile the man.

eyes can endure to behold no iniquity, *Proverbs* xv. 26. as good *meditations are acceptable*, *Psalm* xix. *ult.* so, by the rule of contrary, *bad* are *abominable*.

6. They *hinder* all *good* we should do, and spoil our best performances; vain thoughts draw the heart away in them, that when a man should draw nigh to God, his *heart*, by reason of his thoughts, *is far off from him*, *Isaiah* xxix. 13. *A man's heart goes after his covetousness*, when he should hear, as the Prophet there speaks, *Ezek.* xxxiii. 31, because his thoughts thus run. Now nothing else but sin could separate, and what doth estrange us from God, is sin, and enmity to him.

7. Our thoughts are the *first motioners of all the evil in us.* For they make the motion, and also bring the heart and object together; are panders to our lusts, hold up the object, till the heart hath played the adulterer with it, and committed folly, so in speculative uncleanness, and in other lusts, they hold up the images of those gods the mind creates,

Prov. 15:26 The thoughts of the wicked are an abomination to the LORD: but the words of the pure are pleasant words.

Ps. 19:14 Let the words of my mouth, and the meditation of my heart, be acceptable in thy sight, O LORD, my strength, and my redeemer.

Is. 29:13 Wherefore the Lord said, Forasmuch as this people draw near me with their mouth, and with their lips do honour me, but have removed their heart far from me, and their fear toward me is taught by the precept of men

Ez. 33:31 And they come unto thee as the people cometh, and they sit before thee as my people, and they hear thy words, but they will not do them: for with their mouth they shew much love, but their heart goeth after their covetousness.

Notes:

which the heart falls down and worships; they present credit, riches, beauty, till the heart hath worshipped them, and this, when the things themselves are absent.

To come now to those *particulars* wherein this *vanity or sinfulness* of the *thinking,* meditating power of the mind consists.

First, I will discover it in regard of *thinking what is good,* how unable and loth it is, to good thoughts; and secondly, in regard of the readiness *of it to think of evil and vain things.*

For the first, first in *a want of ability* ordinarily, and naturally to raise and extract holy and useful considerations and thoughts from all ordinary occurrences, and occasions; which the mind, so far as it is sanctified, is apt unto: a heart sanctified, and in whose affections true grace is enkindled, out of all God's dealings with him, out of the things he sees and hears, out of all the objects which are put into the thoughts he distilleth holy and sweet, and useful meditations: and it naturally doth it, and ordinarily doth it, so far as it is sanctified: so our Saviour *Christ*, all speeches of others which he heard, all accidents and occurrences did still raise and occasion in him heavenly meditations, as we may see throughout the whole Gospels: when he came by a well, he speaks of the *Water of life*, *John* iv. &c. many instances might be given; *He* in his thoughts translated the book of the creatures, into the book of grace, and so did *Adam's* heart in innocency: his *Philosophy* might be truly termed *Divinity*, because he saw God in all; all raised up his heart to thankfulness and praise: so now in like manner our minds, so far as they are sanctified, will do. As the *Philosopher's stone* turns all Metals into Gold; as the Bee sucks honey out of every flower, and a good stomach sucks out some sweet and wholesome nourishment out of what it takes into itself: so doth a holy heart, so far as sanctified, convert and digest all into spiritual useful thoughts; this you may see, *Psalm* cvii. *ult. that Psalm* gives many instances of God's providence, *and*

Jn. 4:14 But whosoever drinketh of the water that I shall give him shall never thirst; but the water that I shall give him shall be in him a well of water springing up into everlasting life.
Ps. 107:23-31 They that go down to the sea in ships, that do business in great waters; These see the works of the LORD, and his wonders in the deep. For he commandeth, and raiseth the stormy wind, which lifteth up the waves thereof. They mount up to the heaven, they go down again to the depths: their soul is melted because of trouble. They reel to and fro, and stagger like a drunken man, and are at their wits' end. Then they cry unto the LORD in their trouble, and he bringeth them out of their distresses. He maketh the storm a calm, so that the waves thereof are still. Then are they glad because they be quiet; so he bringeth them unto their desired haven. Oh that men would praise the LORD for his goodness, and for his wonderful works to the children of men!

wonderful works which he doth for the sons of men; as deliverances by Sea, where men see his wonders: deliverance to Captives, &c. and still the foot of the Song is, *Oh that men would therefore praise the Lord for the wonderful works he doth for the sons of men.* Now after all these instances, he concludes, that though others pass over such occurrences with ordinary slight thoughts, yet says he, *the righteous shall see it, and rejoice:* that is, extract comfortable thoughts out of all, which shall be matter of joy, and *who-so is wise will observe those things,* that is, make holy observations out of all these, and out of a principle of wisdom he understands God's goodness in all, and so his heart is raised to thoughts of praise, and thankfulness, and obedience. Now compare with this the xcii. *Psalm,* made for the *Sabbath* when in imitation of God, who that day viewed his works, we are, on our *Lord's day,* still to raise holy praiseful thoughts out of them to his glory, (which he that penned that *Psalm* then did, *ver.* 1,

Ps. 107:42-43 The righteous shall see it, and rejoice: and all iniquity shall stop her mouth. Whoso is wise, and will observe these things, even they shall understand the lovingkindness of the LORD.

Ps. 92:1-2 It is a good thing to give thanks unto the LORD, and to sing praises unto thy name, O most High: To shew forth thy lovingkindness in the morning, and thy faithfulness every night

and 2,) and *ver.* 5, *how great are thy works, &c.! a brutish man knows not, nor will a fool understand this:* that is, he, an unregenerate man being as a beast, and having no sanctified principle of wisdom in him, looks no further than a beast into all the works of God, and occurrences of things; looks on all blessings as things provided for man's delight by God: but he extracts seldom holy spiritual and useful thoughts out of all, he wants the art of doing it.

If injuries be offered us by others, what do our thoughts distil out of those wrongs, but thoughts of revenge? we meditate how to requite it again. But see how naturally *David's* mind distils other thoughts of *Shimei's* cursing, ii. *Sam.* 16, 11. *God hath bidden him,* and it may prove a good sign of God's favor, *God may requite good for it;* when we see judgments befal others, severe thoughts of censure our minds are apt to raise against our brother, as *Job's* friends did. But a godly man whose mind is much sanctified, raiseth other thoughts out

Ps. 92:5-6 O LORD, how great are thy works! and thy thoughts are very deep. A brutish man knoweth not; neither doth a fool understand this.
2 Sam. 16:11-12 And David said to Abishai, and to all his servants, Behold, my son, which came forth of my bowels, seeketh my life: how much more now may this Benjamite do it? let him alone, and let him curse; for the LORD hath bidden him. It may be that the LORD will look on mine affliction, and that the LORD will requite me good for his cursing this day.

of it, *Prov.* xxi. 12, *wisely considers, &c.*

So when outward mercies befall us, the next thoughts we are apt to have, is to project ease by our wealth, thou *hast goods for many years*: and when judgments befall us, we are apt to be filled with thoughts of complaint, and fears, and cares how to wind out again. But what were the first thoughts *Job* had, upon the news of the loss of all? *God hath given, and the Lord hath taken, blessed be the Lord for all.*

Such thoughts as these (which all opportunities hint unto) a good heart is apprehensive of, and doth naturally raise for its own use: so far *barren as our thoughts are, so far vain.*

Secondly, the *vanity,* and sinfulness of the mind appears in a *loathness* to *entertain holy thoughts,* to begin to set itself to think of God, and the things belonging unto our peace; even as loath they are to this, as School-boys are to go to their books, or to busy their minds about their lessons, their heads being full of play; so loath are our

Prov. 21:12 The righteous man wisely considereth the house of the wicked: but God overthroweth the wicked for their wickedness.
Lk. 12:19 And I will say to my soul, Soul, thou hast much goods laid up for many years; take thine ease, eat, drink, and be merry.
Job 1:21 And said, Naked came I out of my mother's womb, and naked shall I return thither: the LORD gave, and the LORD hath taken away; blessed be the name of the LORD.

minds to enter into serious considerations, into sad solemn thoughts of God or death, &c. men are as loath to think of *death*, as thieves of the *assizes and execution;* or to think of *God,* as they are of their Judge: so to go over their own actions, in a review of them, and read the blurd writing of their hearts, and to *commune with them,* at night in the end of the day, (as *David* did, *Psalm* cxix. 59), men are as loath to do this, as School-boys are to parse their lessons, and the false Latins they have made, *Job* xxi. 14, *Depart from us* (say they in Job) unto God, (from their thoughts they meant it), *for* it follows, *we desire not the knowledge of thy ways:* they would not think of him, or know them by their good wills; and there-fore our minds, like a bad stomach, are nauseated with the very scent of good things, and soon casts them up again, *Romans* i. 28. *They like not to retain the knowledge of God:* let us go and try to wind up our souls, at any time, to holy meditations, to think of what we have heard, or what we

Ps. 119:59 I thought on my ways, and turned my feet unto thy testimonies.
Job 21:14 Therefore they say unto God, Depart from us; for we desire not the knowledge of thy ways.
Rom. 1:28 And even as they did not like to retain God in their knowledge, God gave them over to a reprobate mind, to do those things which are not convenient

have done, or what is our duty to do, and we shall find our minds, like the pegs of an Instrument, slip between our fingers, as we are a winding them up, and to fall down suddenly again, e're we are aware of it: yea you shall find, that your minds will labour to shun what may occasion such thoughts; even as men go out of the way, when they see they must meet with one they are loath to speak withal; yea hence 'tis that men dare not be alone, for fear such thoughts should return upon them: the best shall find a gladness, for an excuse, by other occasions to knock off their thoughts from what is good: whereas in thinking of vain earthly things, we think the time passeth too fast, clocks strike too soon, hours pass away e're we are aware of it.

Thirdly, the *vanity* and sinfulness of the mind appears in the godly, that though they entertain good thoughts, yet the mind is not, will not be *long intent* on them. Some things there are, which we are, and can be intent upon, and accordingly dwell long upon them, and therefore in *Job* xvii. 11. *the thoughts* are called the *possessions of the heart,* (so 'tis in the original, and noted in the margin) such thoughts as are pleasing, the heart dwells on them ; yea so intent are we often, that they hinder our sleep: as 'tis said of wicked men, *they cannot sleep for multitude of thoughts, Eccles.* v. 12, *so to devise froward things, Solomon* says, *Prov.* xvi. 30, *that a man shuts his eyes,* that is, is exceeding attentive, poreth upon his plots; for so a man doth use to do, to shut his eyes when he would be intent, and therefore it is so expressed. But now let the mind be occupied and busied about good things, and things belonging to our peace, how unsteady is it ? which things should yet draw out the highest intention of the mind: for the more excellent the object is, the stronger our intention should be. God is the most glorious object our minds can fasten on, the most alluring, the thought of whom therefore should swallow up all other, as not worthy to be seen the same day with Him :

Job 17:11 My days are past, my purposes are broken off, even the thoughts of my heart.
Ecc. 5:12 The sleep of a labouring man is sweet, whether he eat little or much: but the abundance of the rich will not suffer him to sleep.
Prov. 16:30 He shutteth his eyes to devise froward things: moving his lips he bringeth evil to pass.

but I appeal to all your experiences, if your thoughts of Him be not most unsteady, and are, (that I may so compare it) as when we look upon a Star through an optique glass, held with a palsy shaking hand: it is long ere we can bring our minds to have ken of him, to place our eyes upon him, and when we have, how do our hands shake, and so lose sight ever and anon? so whilst we are in never so serious talk with Him, when all things else should stand without, and not dare to offer entrance, till we have done with Him, yet how many chinks are there in the heart, at which other thoughts come in? and our minds leave God, and follow them, and *go after our covetousness,* our credit &c. as the Prophet's phrase is, *Ezek.* xxxiii. 31, so when we are hearing the Word, how do our minds ever and anon run out of the Church, and come in again, and so do not hear half that is said? so when we are at our callings, which God bids us to be conversant about with all our might, *Eccles.* ix. 10, yet our minds like idle truants or negligent

Ez. 33:31 And they come unto thee as the people cometh, and they sit before thee as my people, and they hear thy words, but they will not do them: for with their mouth they shew much love, but their heart goeth after their covetousness.
Ecc. 9:10 Whatsoever thy hand findeth to do, do it with thy might; for there is no work, nor device, nor knowledge, nor wisdom, in the grave, whither thou goest.

servants, though sent about never so serious a business, yet go out of the way to see any sport, run after the Hares that cross the way, follow after Butterflies that buzz about us.

And so when we come to pray, Christ bids *watch and pray, Mark* xiii. 33, which is spoken as if we were at every door to place a guard that none come in and disturb and knock us off: but how oft doth the heart nod, and fall asleep, and run into another world, as men in dreams do? yea so natural are distractions to us, when we are busied about holy duties, that we are carried out of that stream of good our mind was running in, into some by-creek ere we are aware of it.

Fourthly, the *vanity* of the mind in our thoughts appears, in regard of *good* things, that if it doth think of them, yet it doth it *unseasonably*. It is with your thoughts as with your speeches, their goodness lies in their placing and order, *Prov.* xxv. 11. *If fitly spoken*, they are *as apples of Gold in pictures of Silver*. And as a

Mk. 13:33 Take ye heed, watch and pray: for ye know not when the time is.
Prov. 25:11 A word fitly spoken is like apples of gold in pictures of silver.

man is to bring forth actions, so thoughts in *due season;* as those *fruits,* so these *buds* should come out in *season, Psalm* i. 3, now the vanity of the mind appears in thinking of some good things sometimes unseasonably; when you are praying, you should not only have no worldly thoughts come in, but no other than praying thoughts: but then haply some notions of, or for a Sermon will come readily in: so in hearing, a man shall often have good thoughts that are utterly hetero-geneal to the thing in hand; so when a man is falling down to prayer, look what thing a man had forgotten, when it should have been thought of, will then come in, or what will affect a man much, comes in to divert him and whirl his thoughts another way; this *misplacing* of *thoughts* (suppose they be good) is yet from a vanity of the mind; did those thoughts come at another time, they should be welcome: we find our minds ready to spend thoughts about any thing, rather than what God at present calls unto: when we go to hear a Sermon, we find we

Ps. 1:3 And he shall be like a tree planted by the rivers of water, that bringeth forth his fruit in his season; his leaf also shall not wither; and whatsoever he doeth shall prosper.

could then spend our thoughts more willingly about reading, or searching our hearts; which at another time, when called to it, we should be most unwilling to: we could be content to run wild over the fields of meditations, and miscellaneous thoughts, though about good, rather than to be tied to a task, and kept in one set path.

In *Adam* and *Christ* no thought was misplaced, but though they were as *many* as the *Stars*, yet they marched in their *courses*, and kept their ranks: but ours, as Meteors, dance up and down in us: and this *disorder* is a *vanity* and *sin*, be the thought materially never so good: not every one that hath the best part must therefore first step upon the Stage to act, but take his right cue. In Printing, let the letters be never so fair, yet if not placed in their order, and rightly composed, they mar the sense: soldiers, upon no terms should break their ranks: so nor should our thoughts; in *Proverbs* xvi. 3, there is a promise to a *Righteous man, that* (as some read it) *his thoughts shall be*

Prov. 16:3 Commit thy works unto the LORD, and thy thoughts shall be established.

ordered: so much for the first part; *the privative* sinfulness in our *thoughts,* in respect of *what is good.*

Now secondly, I proceed to discover that *positive vanity,* which appeareth in our thoughts, in regard of *what is evil;* and here it is not to be expected, nor indeed can it be performed by any man, to reckon up the several particularities of all those vain thoughts which run through man's heart; I will insist only on some more general discoveries, to which particulars may be reduced for a taste of the rest.

First, the *vanity* of them discovers its self, in that which Christ calls, *Mark* vii. 22. ἀφροσύνη, *foolishness:* that is, such thoughts as mad men have, and fools; which *foolishness* is seen, both in that unsettled wantonness and *unstayedness* of the mind in thinking, that like quick-silver it cannot fix, but as *Solomon* says, *Proverbs* xvii. 24. *A fool's eyes are in the ends of the earth,* are garish, and run up and down from one end of the earth to the other, shooting and streaming,

Mk. 7:22 Thefts, covetousness, wickedness, deceit, lasciviousness, an evil eye, blasphemy, pride, foolishness

Prov. 17:24 Wisdom is before him that hath understanding; but the eyes of a fool are in the ends of the earth.

as those Meteors you see sometimes in the air: and though indeed the mind of man is nimble and able thus to run from one end of the earth to another, (which is its strength and excellency) yet God would not have this strength and nimbleness, and metal-spirit shewn in curvetting, and tumbling, (as I may call it) but in steady directing all our thoughts straight on to his glory, our own salvation, and the good of others: he gave it this nimbleness to turn away from evil, and the first appearance of it: as we are to walk in God's ways, he calls us to, so every thought, as well as every action is a step: and therefore ought to be steady, *make straight steps to your feet*, says the Apostle, *Hebrews* xii. 13, turning not to the right hand, nor to the left, until we come to the journey's end of that business we are to think of: but our thoughts, at best, are as wanton spaniels, who though indeed they go with, and accompany their Master, and come to their journey's end with him in the end, yet do run after every

Heb. 12:13 And make straight paths for your feet, lest that which is lame be turned out of the way; but let it rather be healed.

Bird, and wildly pursue every flock of sheep they see: this unsteadiness, it ariseth from the like curse on the mind of *Man*, as was on *Cain*, that being *driven from the presence of the Lord*, it proves a vagabond, *and so men's eyes are in the ends of the earth.*

This foolishness or ἀφροσύνη is also seen in that *independence* in our thoughts; they hanging oft together as ropes of sand; this we see more evidently in dreams: and not only then, but when awake also, and *that*, when we would set ourselves to be most serious, how do our thoughts jangle and ring backward! and as wanton Boys, when they take pens in their hands, scribble broken words that have no dependence: thus do our thoughts: and if you would but look over the copies thereof, which you write continually, you would find as much nonsense in your thoughts, as you find in mad men's speeches. This madness and distemper is in the mind since the fall (though it appears not in our words, because we are wiser) that if notes were taken of our thoughts,

Gen. 4:14 Behold, thou hast driven me out this day from the face of the earth; and from thy face shall I be hid; and I shall be a fugitive and a vagabond in the earth; and it shall come to pass, that every one that findeth me shall slay me.

_____

_____

_____

_____

_____

_____

_____

_____

_____

_____

_____

_____

_____

we should find thoughts so vagrant, that we know not how they come nor whence they came, nor whither they would. But as *God* doth *all things in weight, number,* and *measure,* so doth his Image in us, so far as it is renewed: and by reason of these two, the *folly, unsettledness,* and *independence* of our thoughts, we bring our thoughts often to no issue, to no perfection, but wilder away our time *in thinking* (as you use to say) *of nothing,* and as *Seneca* says of men's *lives,* as of Ships that are tossed up and down at Sea, it may be said they have been *tossed much,* but *sailed* nothing. The like in this respect may be said of our thoughts, or as when men make imperfect dashes, and write nonsense, *they are said to scribble, they do not write:* so in these follies and independencies, we wilder and *loose ourselves, we do not think.*

But secondly, on the contrary, if any *strong lust,* or violent passion be up, then our thoughts are *too fixed* and *intent,* and run in so far into such sinful objects, that

Prov. 16:11 A just weight and balance are the LORD'S: all the weights of the bag are his work.

they cannot be pulled out again, or any way diverted or taken off: which is another vanity. For our thoughts and our understanding part was ordained to moderate, allay, and cool, and take off our passions when they are a playing over, to rule and govern them. But now our thoughts are themselves subjected to our affections, and like fuel put under them, do but make them boil the more : and although our thoughts do first stir up our fears, joys, desires, &c. yet these being stirred up once, chain, and fix, and hold our thoughts to those objects, so as we cannot loosen them again. Therefore says Christ to his Disciples, *why are you troubled, and why do thoughts arise in your hearts?* for perturbations in the affections cause thoughts like fumes, and vapours to ascend. Thus if a *passion of fear* be up, how doth it conjure up multitude of ghostly thoughts which we cannot conjure down again, nor hide our eyes from? but which like ghosts haunt us, and follow us up and down, where-ever we go, so as a

Lk. 24:38-39 And he said unto them, Why are ye troubled? and why do thoughts arise in your hearts? Behold my hands and my feet, that it is I myself: handle me, and see; for a spirit hath not flesh and bones, as ye see me have.

man runs away pursued by his own thoughts, *the heart then meditates on terror*. *Isaiah* xxxiii. 18, so when sorrow is up, how doth it make us study the cross that lights upon us? which to forget, would be an ease unto the mind. But a man's passions make his thoughts to con it, and to say it by heart, over and over again, as if it would not have us forget it: so when *love or desire* is up, be the thing what it will we are taken with, as preferment, credit, beauty, riches, it sets our thoughts awork to view the thing all over, from top to toe (as we say) to observe every part and circumstance, that doth make it amiable unto us: as if a picture were to be drawn of it. So when *joy* is up, we view the thing we rejoice in, and read it over and over; as we do a Book we like, and we mark every tittle, we are punctual in it; yea so inordinate are we herein, as often we cannot sleep for thinking of them, *Eccles.* v. 12. *Abundance of riches will not suffer him to sleep, for the multitude of thoughts in his head*, speaking of a man who is covetous:

Is. 33:18 Thine heart shall meditate terror. Where is the scribe? where is the receiver? where is he that counted the towers?
Ecc. 5:12 The sleep of a labouring man is sweet, whether he eat little or much: but the abundance of the rich will not suffer him to sleep.

how do thoughts trouble the *Belshazzars,* and *Nebuchadnezzars* of the world? *Daniel* iv. 19, so *Proverbs* iv. 16. *They sleep not unless they have done mischief,* if their desires remain unsatisfied, they do disturb their thoughts, like froward children by their crying: so as often, *these* which men count *free* (as the most do *thoughts*) do prove the greatest bondage and torment in the earth unto them, and do hinder sleep, the nurse of nature, eat out, and live upon the heart that bred them, weary the spirits, that when a man *shall say* (as *Job* vii. 13), *my bed shall comfort me,* by putting a parenthesis to his thoughts, and sad discourses, which he hath when awake, yet then they haunt a man; and as *verse* 14, *terrify him.* A man cannot lay them aside as he doth his cloak: and when men die they will follow them to hell, and torment them worse there; your thoughts are some of the greatest executioners there, even the *worm that dies not.*

Thirdly, the *vanity* of the mind appears in *curiosity;* a longing and itching to be fed

---

Dan. 4:19 Then Daniel, whose name was Belteshazzar, was astonied for one hour, and his thoughts troubled him. The king spake, and said, Belteshazzar, let not the dream, or the interpretation thereof, trouble thee. Belteshazzar answered and said, My lord, the dream be to them that hate thee, and the interpretation thereof to thine enemies.
Prov. 4:16 For they sleep not, except they have done mischief; and their sleep is taken away, unless they cause some to fall.
Job 7:13-14 When I say, My bed shall comfort me, my couch shall ease my complaint; Then thou scarest me with dreams, and terrifiest me through visions
Mk. 9:46 Where their worm dieth not, and the fire is not quenched.

with, and to know (and then delighting to think of) things that do not at all concern us: take an experiment of this in Scholars, (whose chief work lies in this shop) how many precious thoughts are spent this way? as in curiosity of knowledge, as appears by those the Apostle often rebukes, that affect, as 1 *Tim.* vi. 4, 20, *oppositions of science falsely so called* curiosities of knowledge *of things they have not seen:* so *Col.* ii. 8, and 1 *Tim.* iv. 7, he calls such issues of men's brains they dote on, *old wives' fables;* because as fables please old wives, so do these their minds, and of that itch they have in them, even as women with child, in their longings, content not themselves with what the place affords, or the season, with what may be had; but often long after some unheard of rarity, far fetched, or, it may be, not at all to be had: thus men not contenting themselves with the wonders of God, discovered in the depth of his Word and Works, they will launch into another Sea, and world of their own making, and here they sail with

1 Tim. 6:4,20 He is proud, knowing nothing, but doting about questions and strifes of words, whereof cometh envy, strife, railings, evil surmisings,... O Timothy, keep that which is committed to thy trust, avoiding profane and vain babblings, and oppositions of science falsely so called

Col. 2:8 Beware lest any man spoil you through philosophy and vain deceit, after the tradition of men, after the rudiments of the world, and not after Christ.

1 Tim. 4:7 But refuse profane and old wives' fables, and exercise thyself rather unto godliness.

pleasure, as many of the School-men did in some of their speculations, spending their precious wits in framing curious webs out of their own bowels.

Take another instance also in others, who have leisure and parts to read much, they should ballast their hearts with the Word, and take in those more precious words of wisdom, and sound knowledge to profit themselves and others, and to build up their own souls; or such studies whereby they may be enabled to serve their Country: but now what do their curious fancies carry them unto, to be versed in, but Play-books, jeering Pasquils, Romances, feigned Stories, which are the curious needlework of idle brains, they load their heads with *Apes and Peacock's feathers*, instead of pearls, and precious stones; so as a man may say as *Solomon, Proverbs* xv. 14. *The heart of him that hath understanding seeketh knowledge, but the mouth of fools feeds on foolishness:* foolish discourses please their ears and eyes to read: all these being but purveyors (as it

Prov. 15:14 The heart of him that hath understanding seeketh knowledge: but the mouth of fools feedeth on foolishness.

_____

_____

_____

_____

_____

_____

_____

_____

_____

_____

_____

_____

_____

were) for food for the thoughts; like Chameleons, men live on air and wind.

To leave them, how do others out of mere curiosity to know and please their thoughts, listen after all the news that flies up and down the world, scum all the froth that floats in foolish men's mouths, and please themselves only with talking, thinking, and hearing of it.

I do not condemn all herein: some, their ends are good, and they can make use of it, and do as *Nehemiah* did, who inquired how things went at *Jerusalem*, to rejoice with God's people, and mourn with them, and pray for them, and to know how to fashion their prayers accordingly: but I condemn that curious itch that is in men, when it is done, but merely to please their fancies, which is much delighted with new things, though they concern us not; such the Athenians were, *Acts* xvii. 21. How do some men long all the week, till they hear events and issues, and make it a great part of the happiness of their lives, to study the

Neh. 1:2-4 That Hanani, one of my brethren, came, he and certain men of Judah; and I asked them concerning the Jews that had escaped, which were left of the captivity, and concerning Jerusalem. And they said unto me, The remnant that are left of the captivity there in the province are in great affliction and reproach: the wall of Jerusalem also is broken down, and the gates thereof are burned with fire. And it came to pass, when I heard these words, that I sat down and wept, and mourned certain days, and fasted, and prayed before the God of heaven

Acts 17:21 (For all the Athenians and strangers which were there spent their time in nothing else, but either to tell, or to hear some new thing.)

state more than their own hearts, and affairs of their callings: who take actions of state as their text, to study the meaning of, and to preach on where-ever they come. I speak of those that yet lay not to heart the miseries of the Church of Christ, nor help them with their prayers, if at any time they happen.

The like curiosity is seen in many, in desiring to know the secrets of other men, which yet would do them no good to know, and who do study men's actions and ends, not to reform, or do good to them, but to know them, and think and muse thereof, when alone, with pleasure; this is curiosity, and properly a vanity of the thinking power, which it mainly pleaseth; this is indeed a great sin, when much of men's most pleasing thoughts are spent on things concern them not: for the things we ought to know, and which do concern us, are enough to take up all our thoughts alone, neither shall we have any to spare: and thoughts are precious things, the immediate fruits and buds of an immortal nature, and God hath given us power to coin them, in order to lay them out in things that concern our own good, and of our neighbours, and His own glory: and thus not to spend them is the greatest waste in the world; examine what Corn you put in to grind, for God ought to have toll of all. *Proverbs* xxiv. 8, *he that deviseth evil, shall be called a mischievous person,* not always he that doth a mischievous action, but that deviseth it: and verse 9, he aggravates it, *à minori, for every thought is sin,* then a combination and conspiracy of wicked thoughts is much more.

But fourthly, there is a worse *vanity* than this, and that is, that intimated, *Romans* xiii. ult. *Taking thought to fulfil the lusts of the flesh,* πρόνοιαν ποιεῖσθαι (*to make projects for it*). For thoughts are the Caterers for our lusts, and lay in all their provision, they are they that look out where the best markets are, the best opportunities for sinning in any kind, the best bargains for credit, for preferment, for riches, &c. for example, would

Prov. 24:8-9 He that deviseth to do evil shall be called a mischievous person. The thought of foolishness is sin: and the scorner is an abomination to men.
Rom. 13:14 But put ye on the Lord Jesus Christ, and make not provision for the flesh, to fulfil the lusts thereof.

a man rise? his thoughts study the art of it, men frame their own ladder to climb withal, invent ways how to do it, though often it proves as to *Haman* their own Gallows. Would they be rich? what do they study? even all cheats and tricks on the Cards, (as I may so speak) that is, all the cunning tricks of the world, all the ways of oppressing, defrauding, and going beyond their brethren, so to pack things in all their dealings, that they themselves shall be the winners, and those that deal with them, the losers, *Isaiah* xxxii. 7. It is said, *that the Instruments of the churlish are evil, and he deviseth wicked devices to destroy the poor*: would a man undermine his opposite, as one that stands in his light, and who hinders his credit? he'll dig and fall a pioning, with his thoughts, his engines, in the night, dig a pit, as the *Scripture phrase is*, and dig deep to hide his counsel, to blow him up in the end, and so as he shall not know who hurt him; and this is worse than all the former, this studied artificial villany.

Est. 7:10 So they hanged Haman on the gallows that he had prepared for Mordecai. Then was the king's wrath pacified.
Is. 32:7 The instruments also of the churl are evil: he deviseth wicked devices to destroy the poor with lying words, even when the needy speaketh right.
Ps. 7:15 He made a pit, and digged it, and is fallen into the ditch which he made.

The more devising there is in sin, the worse: therefore the fact about *Uriah*, not so much that of *Bathsheba*, is objected against *David*, because he used art in it; he *took thought for it*, but in the matter of *Bathsheba, thoughts took him*.

Fifthly, the *representing* or acting *over sins*, in our thoughts and imaginations, personating those pleasures by imagination, which at present we enjoy not really, feigning and imagining ourselves to act those sinful practices we have not opportunity outwardly to perform: *speculative wickedness* Divines do call it, which to be in the power of imagination to do, is evident to you by your dreams; when fancy plays its part most, and to allude to what the Prophet says, makes us believe *we eat when we are an hungry, to drink when our souls are thirsty, Isaiah* xxix. 8: but I mean not to speak of the power and corruption of it, as in our dreams: it were well if, as the Apostle speaks of *Drunkenness*, that this speculative wickedness were only *in the night:* but

Is. 29:8 It shall even be as when an hungry man dreameth, and, behold, he eateth; but he awaketh, and his soul is empty: or as when a thirsty man dreameth, and, behold, he drinketh; but he awaketh, and, behold, he is faint, and his soul hath appetite: so shall the multitude of all the nations be, that fight against mount Zion.

corrupt and distempered affections do cast men into such dreams in the day, and when they are awake, there are then (to borrow the Apostle's expression) *filthy dreams, Jude* xiii. *that defile the flesh,* even when awake: when, their lusts wanting work, their fancy erects to them a stage, and they set their imaginations and thoughts a work to entertain their filthy and impure desires, with shows and plays of their own making, and so *reason,* and the intention of their minds, sit as spectators all the while to view with pleasure, till their thoughts inwardly act over their own unclean desires, ambitious projects, or what ever else they have a mind unto: so *vain* and empty is the heart of man become, so *impatient* are our desires and lusts of interruption in their pleasures, so sinful and corrupt.

First, vain and empty it appears to be in this; for take all the pleasures of sin, when they are never so fully, solidly, really, and substantially enjoyed, they are but shadows, a mere outside and figure, as the Apostle

Jude 8 Likewise also these filthy dreamers defile the flesh, despise dominion, and speak evil of dignities.

_____

_____

_____

_____

_____

_____

_____

_____

_____

_____

_____

_____

calls the world : it is opinion of imagination that casts that varnish of goodness on them, which is not truly in them : so *Felix* and *Bernice's* pomp is termed πολυφαντασία ; but now this speculative enjoying of them only in imagination, (which many men's hearts take so much pleasure in), the pleasing ourselves in the bare thoughts and imaginations of them, this is but a shadow of these shadows, that the soul should *Ixion* like embrace and commit adultery with clouds only ; this is a *vanity* beyond all other vanities, that maketh us vainer than other creatures, who though *subject* to *vanity*, yet not to such as this.

Secondly, it argues our desires to be impatient, to be detained from, or interrupted of their pleasures: when the soul shall be found so greedy, that when the heart is debarred or sequestered from those things it desires, and wants means or opportunities to act its lusts, as not being to stay, it will at least enjoy them in imagination, and in the *interim*, set fancy to entertain the mind with empty

Rom. 8:20 For the creature was made subject to vanity, not willingly, but by reason of him who hath subjected the same in hope

pictures of them drawn in its own thoughts.

Thus, thirdly, they appear also to be exceeding sinful and corrupt; an *outward* act of sin is but as an act of *Whoredom* with the creature, when *really* enjoyed: but this is *Incest*, when we defile our souls and spirits with these imaginations and likenesses which are begotten in our own fancies, being the children of our own hearts.

And yet (my brethren) such speculative enjoying of pleasures, and acting over of sins the mind of man is full of, as will appear in many particulars.

First, look what comforts men have *at present* in their possession, and at command, what *excellencies* or endowments, men love to be alone to study, and think of them, and when they are sequestered from the present use of them, yet they will then be again and again recounting and casting of them up, taking a survey of their happiness in them, applauding their own hearts in their conditions: and as rich men, that love money, love to be looking on it, and telling it over; so do men to be summing up their comforts and privileges they enjoy, which others want; as, how rich they are, how great, how they excel others in parts and gifts, &c. Oh how much of that precious sand of our thoughts runs out this way! thus he in the Gospel, he keeps an audit in his heart; *Soul* (saith he) *thou hast goods laid up for many years:* so *Haman. Esther* v. 11, takes an Inventory of his honours and goods, he talks *of all the glory of his riches, and all the things wherein the King had promoted him*: so *Nebuchadnezzar, Daniel* iv. 30, as it may seem, he was alone walking and talking to himself, like a fool, saying to himself; *is not this great Babylon, which I have built by the might of my power, for the glory of my Majesty?*

And as thus upon their comforts, so also upon their excellencies, as their learning, wisdom, parts, &c. men love to stand looking upon these in the glass of their own speculation, as fair faces love to look often and

Lk. 12:19 And I will say to my soul, Soul, thou hast much goods laid up for many years; take thine ease, eat, drink, and be merry.

Es. 5:11 And Haman told them of the glory of his riches, and the multitude of his children, and all the things wherein the king had promoted him, and how he had advanced him above the princes and servants of the king.

Dan. 4:30 The king spake, and said, Is not this great Babylon, that I have built for the house of the kingdom by the might of my power, and for the honour of my majesty?

long in Looking-glasses, which, as it ariseth from that self-flattery is in men; so also that they might keep their happiness still fresh and continued in their eye; which thoughts, when they raise not up the heart to thankfulness to God, and are not used to that end, but are bellows of pride; they are vain and abominable in the *eyes* of God, as appears by God's dealing with those fore-mentioned; for to the one he says, *thou fool, this night;* the other *whilst the word was in his mouth,* (giving him no longer warning) he strikes with madness and bru-tishness: and *Haman,* you know, was like a *Wall* that doth *swell* before it *breaks,* and falls to ruin and decay.

Secondly, *this speculative* enjoying of pleasures, and acting over sins thus in fancy, doth appear in regard *of things to come;* which when we have in view, or any hopes of, men's thoughts go forth before to meet them; with how much contentment do men's thoughts entertain their desires, with vain promisings and expectations aforehand of

Lk. 12:20 But God said unto him, Thou fool, this night thy soul shall be required of thee: then whose shall those things be, which thou hast provided?

Dan. 4:31-33 While the word was in the king's mouth, there fell a voice from heaven, saying, O king Nebuchadnezzar, to thee it is spoken; The kingdom is departed from thee. And they shall drive thee from men, and thy dwelling shall be with the beasts of the field: they shall make thee to eat grass as oxen, and seven times shall pass over thee, until thou know that the most High ruleth in the kingdom of men, and giveth it to whomsoever he will. The same hour was the thing fulfilled upon Nebuchadnezzar: and he was driven from men, and did eat grass as oxen, and his body was wet with the dew of heaven, till his hairs were grown like eagles' feathers, and his nails like birds' claws.

their pleasures, that are in view and in possibility to be enjoyed: so they in *Isaiah* wind up their hearts to a higher pin of jollity in the midst of their cups, in that their hearts thought and promised them, *To morrow shall be as to day, and much more abundant, Isaiah* lvi. 12. So they *James* iv. 13, they say with themselves, *we will go to such a City, and continue there a year, and get gain:* and the promise of this, and the thoughts of it aforehand feeds them, and keeps up their hearts in comfort. When men rise in a morning, they begin to forethink with much pleasure, what carnal pleasures they have the advowson and promise of, that day or week, as to go to such company, and there be merry; to go such a pleasant journey, enjoy satisfaction in such a lust, hear such news, &c. and thus as godly men *live by faith* in God's promises, *Hab.* ii. 4. *Isaiah* xxxviii. 16, *by these men live, and this is the spirit of my life,* saith *Hezekiah,* even *what God hath spoken, verse* 15, so do carnal men live much upon

Is. 56:12 Come ye, say they, I will fetch wine, and we will fill ourselves with strong drink; and to morrow shall be as this day, and much more abundant.
Jam. 4:13 Go to now, ye that say, To day or to morrow we will go into such a city, and continue there a year, and buy and sell, and get gain
Hab. 2:4 Behold, his soul which is lifted up is not upright in him: but the just shall live by his faith.
Is. 38:15-16 What shall I say? he hath both spoken unto me, and himself hath done it: I shall go softly all my years in the bitterness of my soul. O Lord, by these things men live, and in all these things is the life of my spirit: so wilt thou recover me, and make me to live.

the promises of their own hearts and thoughts aforehand (for to this head of vain thoughts, these *vain promisings* are to be reduced, *Psalm* xlix. 11). *Their inward thought is, their houses shall continue for ever,* and this thought pleaseth them : what pleasure almost is there, which a man makes much account of, but he acts it first over in private in his own thoughts? and thus do men foolishly take their own words and promises, and so *befool themselves in the end,* as *Jeremiah* speaks, *Jer.* xvii. 11, they take up before hand in their thoughts upon trust, the pleasures they are to enjoy, even as spend-thrifts do their rents, or Heirs their revenues before they come of age to enjoy their lands, that when they come indeed to enjoy the pleasures they expected, either they prove but *dreams,* as *Isaiah* xxix. 8, they find their *souls empty,* or so much under their expectation, and so stale, as they have little in them, that there still proves more in the imagination than in the thing, which ariseth from the vastness and

---

Ps. 49:11 Their inward thought is, that their houses shall continue for ever, and their dwelling places to all generations; they call their lands after their own names.
Jer. 17:11 As the partridge sitteth on eggs, and hatcheth them not; so he that getteth riches, and not by right, shall leave them in the midst of his days, and at his end shall be a fool.
Is. 29:8 It shall even be as when an hungry man dreameth, and, behold, he eateth; but he awaketh, and his soul is empty: or as when a thirsty man dreameth, and, behold, he drinketh; but he awaketh, and, behold, he is faint, and his soul hath appetite: so shall the multitude of all the nations be, that fight against mount Zion.

---

greediness of men's desires, as the cause hereof; for that makes them swallow up all at once: so *Hab.* ii. 5, *enlarging his desires as Hell, he heaps up all Nations, swallows them up in his thoughts*: so an ambitious Scholar doth all preferments that are in his view.

Thirdly, this *speculative wickedness* is exercised in like manner towards *things past*, in recalling namely, and reviving in our thoughts the pleasure of sinful actions passed; when the mind runs over the passages and circumstances of the same sins long since committed, with a new and fresh delight; when men raise up their dead actions, long since buried, in the same likeness they were transacted in, and parley with them, as the Witch and *Saul* did with Satan in *Samuel's* likeness: and whereas they should draw cross lines over them, and blot them out through faith in Christ's blood, they rather copy and write them over again in their thoughts, with the same contentment: so an unclean person can study

Hab. 2:5 Yea also, because he transgresseth by wine, he is a proud man, neither keepeth at home, who enlargeth his desire as hell, and is as death, and cannot be satisfied, but gathereth unto him all nations, and heapeth unto him all people

1 Sam. 28:14 And he said unto her, What form is he of? And she said, An old man cometh up; and he is covered with a mantle. And Saul perceived that it was Samuel, and he stooped with his face to the ground, and bowed himself.

and view over every circumstance passed in such an act, with such a person committed; so a vain-glorious Scholar doth repeat in his thoughts an eminent performance of his, and all such passages therein as were most elegant: and thus men chew the cud upon any speech of commendation uttered by others of them: and all this even as a good heart doth repeat good things heard or read, with the remembrance also of what quickness they had in such and such passages, and with what affections they were warmed, when they heard them; or as a godly man recalls with comfort the actions of a well-past life, as *Hezekiah* did, *Lord I have walked before thee with a perfect heart,* and thereby do also stir and provoke their hearts to the like temper again: so on the contrary do wicked men use to recall, and revive the pleasingest sinful passages in their lives, to suck a new sweetness out of them: than which nothing argues more *hardness* and *wickednesss* of heart, or provokes God more: for,

Lev. 11:3 Whatsoever parteth the hoof, and is clovenfooted, and cheweth the cud, among the beasts, that shall ye eat.

Is. 38:2-3 Then Hezekiah turned his face toward the wall, and prayed unto the LORD, And said, Remember now, O LORD, I beseech thee, how I have walked before thee in truth and with a perfect heart, and have done that which is good in thy sight. And Hezekiah wept sore.

First, it argues much *wickedness* of heart, and such as when it is ordinary with the heart to do thus, is not compatible with grace: for in the vi. of the *Romans, verse* 21, the Apostle shews that a good heart useth to reap no such fruit of sinful actions past, *but what fruit had you of those things whereof ye are now ashamed*: the Saints reap and distil nothing out of all those flowers, but shame and sorrow, and sad sighs: when *Ephraim* remembered his sin, he was *ashamed and repented*; and canst thou in thy thoughts, reap a new harvest and crop of pleasure out of them, again and again?

Secondly, it argues much hardness of heart; nothing being more opposite to the truth and practice of repentance, the foundation of which is to call to mind the sin with shame and sorrow, and to recall it with much more grief, than ever there was pleasure in the committing of it: and whose property is to *hate* the *appearance* of it, and to enflame the heart with *zeal* and revenge

Rom. 6:21 What fruit had ye then in those things whereof ye are now ashamed? for the end of those things is death.
Jer. 31:18 I have surely heard Ephraim bemoaning himself thus; Thou hast chastised me, and I was chastised, as a bullock unaccustomed to the yoke: turn thou me, and I shall be turned; for thou art the LORD my God.
1 Thes. 5:22 Abstain from all appearance of evil.

against it: and thereby it provoketh God exceedingly, our hearts are thereby embrued in a new guilt, we thereby stand to, and make good our former act: even so, by remembering it with pleasure, we provoke God to remember it with a new detestation of it, and so to send down new plagues; who, if we recall it with grief, *would remember it no more:* we shew we take delight to rake in those wounds we have given Christ already; to view *the sins of others* with pleasure, *Romans* i. *ult.* is made more *than to commit them:* but much more to view and revive our own with a fresh delight: and therefore know, that however you may take delight here to repeat to yourselves your old sins, yet that in Hell nothing will gall you more, than the remembrance of them; every circumstance in every sin will then be as a dagger at thy heart: this was the rich man's task and study in Hell, to *remember the good things he had received,* and his sins committed in the abuse of them: and if godly men here be made to *possess*

Heb. 8:12 For I will be merciful to their unrighteousness, and their sins and their iniquities will I remember no more.
Rom. 1:32 Who knowing the judgment of God, that they which commit such things are worthy of death, not only do the same, but have pleasure in them that do them.
Lk. 16:23-25 And in hell he lift up his eyes, being in torments, and seeth Abraham afar off, and Lazarus in his bosom. And he cried and said, Father Abraham, have mercy on me, and send Lazarus, that he may dip the tip of his finger in water, and cool my tongue; for I am tormented in this flame. But Abraham said, Son, remember that thou in thy lifetime receivedst thy good things, and likewise Lazarus evil things: but now he is comforted, and thou art tormented.

_____

_____

_____

_____

_____

_____

_____

_____

_____

_____

_____

_____

_____

the sins of their youth with horror, as *Job, and to have them ever before them,* as *David,* how will wicked men be continually affrighted with them in hell? whose punishment is in a great part set forth to us, by this, *Psalm* l. 21, *I will set them in order before thee.*

Fourthly, the fourth thing wherein this *speculative vanity* appears, is in acting sins upon mere imaginary suppositions; men feign and contrive to themselves, and make a supposition to themselves in their own thoughts, first of what *they would be,* and what *they would do:* men create fool's paradises to themselves, and then walk up and down in them; as, if they had money enough, what pleasures they would have; if they were in such places of preferment, how they would carry themselves: to allude to that *Absalom* said, 2 *Samuel* xv. 4, *Oh if I were a Judge in the Land, I would do this or that, &c.* doing this with a great deal of pleasure, almost as much as those that really enjoy them: this may well be the meaning of that

Job 13:26 For thou writest bitter things against me, and makest me to possess the iniquities of my youth.

Ps. 25:7 Remember not the sins of my youth, nor my transgressions: according to thy mercy remember thou me for thy goodness' sake, O LORD.

Ps. 50:21 These things hast thou done, and I kept silence; thou thoughtest that I was altogether such an one as thyself: but I will reprove thee, and set them in order before thine eyes.

2 Sam. 15:4 Absalom said moreover, Oh that I were made judge in the land, that every man which hath any suit or cause might come unto me, and I would do him justice!

Psalm l. 18, where, of the hypocrite (who outwardly abstains from gross sins) 'tis said, that *he consenteth with the thief, and partaketh with the adulterer*, namely, in his *heart* and *fancy*, supposing himself with them, and so desires to be doing what they do; thus take one who is naturally ambitious (whom both nature, parts and education have all made, but a *Bramble never to rule over the trees*, and hath fixed in a lower sphere, as uncapable of rising higher or being greater, as the earth is of becoming a Star in Heaven, yet) he will take upon him in his own heart, feigning and supposing himself to be, and then act the part of, a great man there, erect a throne, and sit down in it; and thinks with himself what he would do if a King or a great Man, &c. so take a man that is unclean, but now grown old, and a *dry tree*, and so cannot act his lust as formerly, yet his thoughts shall supply what is wanting in his strength or opportunity: and he makes his own heart both Bawd, Brothel-house, Whore, Whore-

Ps. 50:18 When thou sawest a thief, then thou consentedst with him, and hast been partaker with adulterers.
Jud. 9:14 Then said all the trees unto the bramble, Come thou, and reign over us.

———————

———————

———————

———————

———————

———————

———————

———————

———————

———————

———————

———————

———————

monger, and all: so a man that is naturally voluptuous, loves pleasures, but wants means to purchase them, yet his inclinations will please themselves with the thoughts of what mixture and composition of delights he would have; he will set down with himself his bill of fare, how he would have, if he might wish, his cup of pleasure mingled, what ingredients put into it: so a man that is revengeful, and yet wants a sting, yet he pleaseth himself with revengeful thoughts and wishes, and will be making invectives and railing dialogues against him he hates, when he is not by: a man in love, in his fancy he will court his Paramour though absent, he will by his imagination make her present, and so frame solemn set speeches to her.

In a word, let men's inclinations and dispositions be of what kind so ever, and let the impossibilities and improbabilities be never so great of being what they desire; yet in their fancies and thoughts they will discover themselves what they would be. *Totumque quod esse desiderant sibi apud semetipsos cogitationibus depingunt;* men will be drawing Maps of their desires, calculate their own inclinations, cut out a condition of life which fills their hearts, and they please themselves withal; and there is no surer way to know a man's natural inclination than by this.

First, which yet first is as great a folly as any other, imitating children herein; for is it not childish to make clay pies and puppets? what else are such fancies as these? and to be as children acting the parts of Ladies and Mistresses, and yet such *childishness* is in men's hearts.

Secondly, a *vanity* also, because a man sets his heart on *what is not*: the things themselves are not, if a man had them, *Proverbs* xxiii. 5, but to please themselves with suppositions is much worse.

Thirdly, this argues the greatest incontentation of mind that may be, when men will in their own thoughts put themselves into another condition than God ever ordained for them.

Prov. 23:5 Wilt thou set thine eyes upon that which is not? for riches certainly make themselves wings; they fly away as an eagle toward heaven.

USE I.

HAVING discovered the vanity of your thoughts and of your estates thereby, be humbled for them; this I ground upon, *Proverbs* xxx. 32, where *Agur* teacheth us to humble ourselves as well for thoughts as actions. *If thou hast done foolishly in lifting up thy self, or if thou hast thought evil, lay thine hand upon thy mouth*: now as *smiting upon the thigh* is put for repentance and shame and sorrow in *Ephraim, Jeremiah* xxxi. 19, so is *laying the hand* upon the mouth put for greater and deeper humiliation, as arguing full conviction of one's guilt, *Romans* iii. 19, *every mouth must be stopped*: having nothing to say, not to plead and excuse that thoughts are free, and it is impossible to be rid of them, &c. but as

Prov. 30:32 If you have been foolish in exalting yourself, Or if you have devised evil, put your hand on your mouth.

Jer. 31:19 Surely after that I was turned, I repented; and after that I was instructed, I smote upon my thigh: I was ashamed, yea, even confounded, because I did bear the reproach of my youth.

Rom. 3:19 Now we know that what things soever the law saith, it saith to them who are under the law: that every mouth may be stopped, and all the world may become guilty before God.

Ezekiel xvi. 63, *to remember and to be confounded, and never to open thy mouth more, to be vile, and not to answer again*: as *Job* xl. 4, 5, this is to lay thy hand on thy mouth, that is, to humble thy self: and indeed there is much cause, for your thoughts they are the first begotten, and eldest sons of original sin, and therefore *the strength of it,* as *Jacob* called *Reuben* the first-born; yea also, and the *Parents* and begetters of all other sins, their *brethren;* the first plotters and contrivers, and *Ahithophels,* in all the treasons and rebellions of our hearts and lives; the bellows and incendiaries of all inordinate affections; the Panders to all our lusts, that *take thought* to provide for the satisfying of them; the disturbers in all good duties, that interrupt and spoil and fly-blow all our prayers, that they stink in the nostrils of God.

And if their heinousness will nothing move you, consider their number, for they are continually thus: which makes our sins to be in number more than the sands: the

Ez. 16:63 That thou mayest remember, and be confounded, and never open thy mouth any more because of thy shame, when I am pacified toward thee for all that thou hast done, saith the Lord GOD.

Job 40:4-5 Behold, I am vile; what shall I answer thee? I will lay mine hand upon my mouth. Once have I spoken; but I will not answer: yea, twice; but I will proceed no further.

Gen. 49:3 Reuben, thou art my firstborn, my might, and the beginning of my strength, the excellency of dignity, and the excellency of power

2 Sam. 17:1 Moreover Ahithophel said unto Absalom, Let me now choose out twelve thousand men, and I will arise and pursue after David this night

Ps. 66:18 If I regard iniquity in my heart, the Lord will not hear me

Prov. 28:9 He that turneth away his ear from hearing the law, even his prayer shall be abomination.

Ps. 40:12 For innumerable evils have compassed me about: mine iniquities have taken hold upon me, so that I am not able to look up; they are more than the hairs of mine head: therefore my heart faileth me.

———————————

———————————

———————————

———————————

———————————

———————————

———————————

———————————

———————————

———————————

———————————

———————————

———————————

thoughts of *Solomon's* heart were as the Sand, and so ours; not a minute, but as many thoughts pass from us, as in a minute sands do in an Hour-glass; so that suppose, that taken severally, they be the smallest and least of your sins, yet their *multitude* makes them more and heavier than all your other; nothing smaller than a grain of *Sand,* but if there be a heap of them, there is nothing *heavier, Job* vi. 3, *my grief is heavier than the Sand*; suppose they be in themselves, but as Farthing-tokens, in comparison of gross defilements: yet because the Mint never lies still, sleeping nor waking, therefore they make up the greatest part of that treasure of wrath which we are a laying up: and know that God will reckon every Farthing, and in thy punishment bate thee not one vain thought; and that God looks upon our thoughts thus, see but the inditement He brings in against the old world, which stands still upon record, *Genesis* vi. 5, when he pronounced that heavy judgment of destroying the old world, doth He

1 Ki. 4:29 And God gave Solomon wisdom and understanding exceeding much, and largeness of heart, even as the sand that is on the sea shore.
Job 6:3 For now it would be heavier than the sand of the sea: therefore my words are swallowed up.
Gen. 6:5 And GOD saw that the wickedness of man was great in the earth, and that every imagination of the thoughts of his heart was only evil continually.

alledge their murders, adulteries, and gross defilements chiefly as the cause? their *thoughts* rather; which because so many, and so *continually evil,* provoked him more than all their other sins. Go down therefore into thy heart, and consider them well, to humble thee, to make thee vile, and if in one room such a treasure of wickedness be found laid up, what in all those other *Chambers of the belly?* (as *Solomon* calls them); consider them to humble thee, but not for all this their multitude to discourage thee: for God hath *more thoughts of mercy* in Him, than thou hast had of rebellion, *Psalm* xl. 5, *thy thoughts towards us.* (speaking of thoughts of mercy) *are more than can be numbered;* thou begannest but as yesterday to think thoughts of rebellion against him, but his thoughts of mercy have been *from everlasting,* and reach to *everlasting:* and therefore *Isaiah* lv. v. 7, having made mention of *our thoughts, let the unrighteous man forsake his thoughts, and He will have mercy on him;* because this objection of the multitude

Prov. 20:27 The spirit of man is the candle of the LORD, searching all the inward parts of the belly.

Jer. 29:11 For I know the thoughts that I think toward you, saith the LORD, thoughts of peace, and not of evil, to give you an expected end.

Ps. 40:5 Many, O LORD my God, are thy wonderful works which thou hast done, and thy thoughts which are to us-ward: they cannot be reckoned up in order unto thee: if I would declare and speak of them, they are more than can be numbered.

Ps. 103:17 But the mercy of the LORD is from everlasting to everlasting upon them that fear him, and his righteousness unto children's children

Is. 55:7 Let the wicked forsake his way, and the unrighteous man his thoughts: and let him return unto the LORD, and he will have mercy upon him; and to our God, for he will abundantly pardon.

might come in to discourage men from hopes of mercy, therefore purposely he adds *he will multiply to pardon;* and to assure us that he hath thoughts of mercy to out-vie ours of sin, he adds, *for my thoughts exceed yours,* as *Heaven doth the earth.*

USE II.

LET us make for ever conscience of them, so *Job* did, *Job* xxxi. 1, I made a covenant with mine eyes, why should I so much as think upon a Maid? *Solomon* gives in especial charge; *above all keeping,* keep thy heart, *Proverbs* iv. 23.

First, thou art to keep the Lord's day holy, thy *self unspotted from the World; to keep thy brother, to keep all the commandments, but above all to keep thy heart,* and in it *thy thoughts;* for this is the great commandment, because it extends itself (as the foundation)

Is. 55:8-9 For my thoughts are not your thoughts, neither are your ways my ways, saith the LORD. For as the heavens are higher than the earth, so are my ways higher than your ways, and my thoughts than your thoughts.
Job 31:1 I made a covenant with mine eyes; why then should I think upon a maid?
Prov. 4:23 Keep thy heart with all diligence; for out of it are the issues of life.
Jam. 1:27 Pure religion and undefiled before God and the Father is this, To visit the fatherless and widows in their affliction, and to keep himself unspotted from the world.
Matt. 18:15 Moreover if thy brother shall trespass against thee, go and tell him his fault between thee and him alone: if he shall hear thee, thou hast gained thy brother.
Jn. 15:10 If ye keep my commandments, ye shall abide in my love; even as I have kept my Father's commandments, and abide in his love.

unto them all: for as in the same Commandment where murder is forbidden, a malicious thought is also, and so of the rest; so in keeping the thoughts, thou virtually keepest all the Commandments: as original sin is said to be forbidden in all the Commandments, so are thy thoughts taken order for, in all.

Secondly, out of it are the issues of life; thoughts and affections are the spring, speeches and actions the stream: as are our thoughts, so are our affections; for these are the bellows, so also our prayers, so all, for they are in the soul as the spirits in the body, they run through all, move all, act all.

Thirdly, if you look to God, our thoughts are that spot of ground, which He proclaims Himself sole Lord of, and makes it one of his greatest titles, that he *knows them,* and *judgeth them;* kings attempt to rule your tongues, to bind your hands, and rule your actions; but God only your thoughts: by them we chiefly sanctify Him in our hearts, by them we walk with God, and shall we not make conscience of them?

Mk. 7:20-23 And he said, That which cometh out of the man, that defileth the man. For from within, out of the heart of men, proceed evil thoughts, adulteries, fornications, murders, Thefts, covetousness, wickedness, deceit, lasciviousness, an evil eye, blasphemy, pride, foolishness: All these evil things come from within, and defile the man.

1 Ch. 28:9 And thou, Solomon my son, know thou the God of thy father, and serve him with a perfect heart and with a willing mind: for the LORD searcheth all hearts, and understandeth all the imaginations of the thoughts: if thou seek him, he will be found of thee; but if thou forsake him, he will cast thee off for ever.

1 Ki. 8:39 Then hear thou in heaven thy dwelling place, and forgive, and do, and give to every man according to his ways, whose heart thou knowest; (for thou, even thou only, knowest the hearts of all the children of men;)

Fourthly, if you look to the work and *power of grace,* wherein lies it, but in *bringing every thought into obedience?* 2 *Corinthians* x. 5, this is the glory of our religion above all other in the world: wherein lies the difficulty of it, the strictness of it, what makes it so hard a task? but the observing and keeping the thoughts in bounds: wherein lies the difference between sincere-hearted Christians and others? but the keeping of our thoughts, without which, all Religion is but *bodily exercise.* Papists may mumble over their prayers, Hypocrites talk, but this is *Godliness.*

Fifthly, if we look to things we have a care of; if we have a care of speeches, because Christ *hath said, we shall answer for every idle word;* why also for the same reason, should we not have a care of thoughts? which are the *words of the mind,* only they want a shape, to be audible to others, which the tongue gives them, for which you must answer, as well as for words, *Hebrews* iv. 12; 1 *Corinthians* iv. 5. If you

2 Cor. 10:5 Casting down imaginations, and every high thing that exalteth itself against the knowledge of God, and bringing into captivity every thought to the obedience of Christ
Matt. 12:36 But I say unto you, That every idle word that men shall speak, they shall give account thereof in the day of judgment.
Heb. 4:12 For the word of God is quick, and powerful, and sharper than any twoedged sword, piercing even to the dividing asunder of soul and spirit, and of the joints and marrow, and is a discerner of the thoughts and intents of the heart.
1 Cor. 4:5 Therefore judge nothing before the time, until the Lord come, who both will bring to light the hidden things of darkness, and will make manifest the counsels of the hearts: and then shall every man have praise of God.

be careful what companions you have, and whom you lodge in your houses, and who lie in your bosoms, then much more of your thoughts, which *lodge* in your hearts, which are not yours, but God's houses; built for himself, and for Christ and *his Word to dwell in:* seeing also the things you think of, have the most near intimate fellowship and converse with you; and therefore when you think of the Word, it is said to *talk with you, Proverbs* vi. 22, if you be careful of what you eat, because such blood you have, &c. then be careful what you think, thoughts being *pabulum animæ,* as *Tully* calls them. *Thy words did I eat* says *Jeremiah,* speaking of meditating on it.

Sixthly, if you look to the issue of things: what shall be the subject of that great inquest at the Day of Judgment? the *thoughts and counsels,* 1 *Corinthians* iv. 5, and after the Day of Judgment, men's thoughts shall prove their greatest executioners: what are the cords God lashes you with to all eternity? your own thoughts;

Jer. 4:14 O Jerusalem, wash thine heart from wickedness, that thou mayest be saved. How long shall thy vain thoughts lodge within thee?
Ps. 119:11 Thy word have I hid in mine heart, that I might not sin against thee.
Prov. 6:22 When thou goest, it shall lead thee; when thou sleepest, it shall keep thee; and when thou awakest, it shall talk with thee.
Jer. 15:16 Thy words were found, and I did eat them; and thy word was unto me the joy and rejoicing of mine heart: for I am called by thy name, O LORD God of hosts.
1 Cor. 4:5 Therefore judge nothing before the time, until the Lord come, who both will bring to light the hidden things of darkness, and will make manifest the counsels of the hearts: and then shall every man have praise of God.

_____

_____

_____

_____

_____

_____

_____

_____

_____

_____

_____

_____

_____

_____

thoughts accusing, whereby you study over every sin; and every one will be as a dagger, *Isaiah* xxxiii. 18, the *Hypocrite's* torment, is to *meditate terrors,* to study God's wrath, and the Saints' blessedness, and their own sins and misery.

REMEDIES AGAINST VAIN THOUGHTS.

THE first is, to get the heart furnished and enriched with a good stock of sanctified and heavenly knowledge: *for a good man* (saith Christ) *hath a good treasure* in his *Heart, Matthew* xiii. 52, that is, he hath all graces, so many precious truths which are as Gold

Is. 33:18 Thine heart shall meditate terror. Where is the scribe? where is the receiver? where is he that counted the towers?

Matt. 12:35 A good man out of the good treasure of the heart bringeth forth good things: and an evil man out of the evil treasure bringeth forth evil things.

in the Ore, which his thoughts, as the Mint, doth coin and beat out, and which, words bring forth. *A good man, out of the good treasure of his heart, brings forth good things.* If therefore there be not Mines of precious truths hid in the heart, no wonder if our thoughts coin nothing but dross, frothy vain thoughts for want of better materials which should feed the Mint, are wanting; therefore *Solomon* saith, *Wicked men forge*, mint, or hammer *wickedness, Proverbs* vi. 14, so JUNIUS reads it: or if men have store of natural knowledge, and want spiritual useful knowledge to themselves, although in company with others, they may bring forth good things in speeches, yet when alone, their thoughts run not on them; for this, take a place of Scripture, *Deuteronomy* vi. 6, 7, which shews, that laying up the Word in the heart, and being much conversant in it, and getting knowledge out of it, is an effectual means to keep our thoughts well exercised when we are alone: for the end why these words are commanded

Prov. 6:14 Frowardness is in his heart, he deviseth mischief continually; he soweth discord.
Dt. 6:6-7 And these words, which I command thee this day, shall be in thine heart: And thou shalt teach them diligently unto thy children, and shalt talk of them when thou sittest in thine house, and when thou walkest by the way, and when thou liest down, and when thou risest up.

to be laid up in the heart, verse 5, 6, is, as to teach them to others, so to take up our thoughts when we are most retired, and alone, and when a man can do nothing, but barely exercise his mind, in thinking; for when a man is a *riding*, or *walking*, or *lying down*, and rising up, (which are often and usually our most retired times for thoughts, and are wholly spent in them, for many ride alone, and lie alone, &c.) yet then, saith he, thou shalt *talk of the Word*: which command he that is alone cannot do, therefore the *talking* there meant is not only λόγος προφωρικὸς, *outward conference* with others, (though intended) as to talk to thy bedfellow of it, and to thy companion: but suppose thou hast none, then to *talk of it* to thy self, for thoughts are λόγοι ἐνδιάθετοι, *talking of the mind*; and so comparing, *Proverbs* vi. 22, with this place (which will fitly interpret it) it appears; for *Solomon* exhorting to the same duty of *binding the Word to the heart*, useth this motive, which is the fruit thereof, *that when thou awakest, it shall talk with*

Dt. 6:5-6 And thou shalt love the LORD thy God with all thine heart, and with all thy soul, and with all thy might. And these words, which I command thee this day, shall be in thine heart
Prov. 6:22 When thou goest, it shall lead thee; when thou sleepest, it shall keep thee; and when thou awakest, it shall talk with thee.
Prov. 3:3-4 Let not mercy and truth forsake thee: bind them about thy neck; write them upon the table of thine heart: So shalt thou find favour and good understanding in the sight of God and man.

thee, that is, by thy thinking of it, it will talk with thee when thou and it art alone: so as thou shalt not need a better companion, it will be putting in and suggesting something.

Secondly, endeavour to preserve and keep up lively, holy, and spiritual affections in thy heart, and suffer them not to cool; *fall not from thy first love,* nor fear, nor joy in God; or if thou hast grown remiss, endeavour to recover those affections again; for such as your affections are, such necessarily must your thoughts be: and they incline the mind to think of such or such objects as will please them, rather than others; therefore says *David, Psalm* cxix. 97, *how do I love thy Law! it is my meditation day and night:* it was his love to it made him think of it so frequently: so *Malachi* iii. 16, *those that feared the Lord and thought upon his name* are joined: for what we fear we often think of, and also speak of often; therefore it is added; *they spake often one to another; fear* made them *think* much *of his name,* and thinking of it made *them speak of it:*

Rev. 2:4 Nevertheless I have somewhat against thee, because thou hast left thy first love.
Ps. 34:9 O fear the LORD, ye his saints: for there is no want to them that fear him.
Phil. 4:4 Rejoice in the Lord alway: and again I say, Rejoice.
Ps. 119:97 O how love I thy law! it is my meditation all the day.
Mal. 3:16 Then they that feared the LORD spake often one to another: and the LORD hearkened, and heard it, and a book of remembrance was written before him for them that feared the LORD, and that thought upon his name.

such affection, such thoughts, and such speeches, as they both are: and indeed thoughts and affections are *sibi mutuo causæ*, the mutual causes of each other: *whilst I mused, the fire burned, Psalm* xxxix. so that thoughts are the bellows that kindle and enflame affections: and then if they are enflamed, they cause thoughts to boil; therefore men newly converted to God, having new and strong affections, can with more pleasure think of God *than any.*

Thirdly, of all apprehensions else, get thy heart possessed with deep, strong and powerful apprehensions and impressions of *God's Holiness, Majesty, Omnipresence, and Omniscience.* If any thoughts be of power to settle, fix, and draw in the mind of man, they are the *thoughts of God.* What is the reason that the Saints and Angels in Heaven have not a vain thought to eternity, not a wry stroke? his presence fixeth them, their eye is never off Him: take a wanton garish loose spirit, let him be but in the presence of a Superior whom he fears and

Ps. 39:3 My heart was hot within me, while I was musing the fire burned: then spake I with my tongue

Is. 6:3 And one cried unto another, and said, Holy, holy, holy, is the LORD of hosts: the whole earth is full of his glory.

Ps. 104:1 Bless the LORD, O my soul. O LORD my God, thou art very great; thou art clothed with honour and majesty.

Jer. 23:24 Can any hide himself in secret places that I shall not see him? saith the LORD. Do not I fill heaven and earth? saith the LORD.

Ps. 147:5 Great is our Lord, and of great power: his understanding is infinite.

reverenceth, and it consolidates him. *Job* made therefore conscience of his thoughts, that he durst not look awry, *Job* xxxi. 1, 2, because God *sees it*, saith he. This drew in and fastened *David's* thoughts, *Psalm* cxxxix. from the first to the twelfth, he manifests what continual apprehension he had of God's Greatness, Majesty, and Omnipresence; and what effect had this? *when I awake I am even before thee, verse* 18. Look, what objects they are that have most strong and deep impressions in the mind, of those, when a man awaketh, he thinks of first; now such strong impressions had *David's* thoughts of God, that still when he awaked, he was with Him, and therefore we find it by experience to be a means to avoid distractions in prayer, to enlarge a man's thoughts in his preparations before, or at the beginning with a consideration of God's attributes and relations to us: and it will and doth make us serious.

Fourthly, especially do this when thou *awakest*, as *David* did there, *when I awake*

Job 31:1-2 I made a covenant with mine eyes; why then should I think upon a maid? For what portion of God is there from above? and what inheritance of the Almighty from on high?
Ps. 139:1-12 O LORD, thou hast searched me, and known me. Thou knowest my downsitting and mine uprising, thou understandest my thought afar off. Thou compassest my path and my lying down, and art acquainted with all my ways. For there is not a word in my tongue, but, lo, O LORD, thou knowest it altogether. Thou hast beset me behind and before, and laid thine hand upon me. Such knowledge is too wonderful for me; it is high, I cannot attain unto it. Whither shall I go from thy spirit? or whither shall I flee from thy presence? If I ascend up into heaven, thou art there: if I make my bed in hell, behold, thou art there. If I take the wings of the morning, and dwell in the uttermost parts of the sea; Even there shall thy hand lead me, and thy right hand shall hold me. If I say, Surely the darkness shall cover me; even the night shall be light about me. Yea, the darkness hideth not from thee; but the night shineth as the day: the darkness and the light are both alike to thee.
Ps. 139:18 If I should count them, they are more in number than the sand: when I awake, I am still with thee.

I am still with thee. To prevent wind which ariseth from emptiness, men use to take a good draught in the morning, on which the stomach feeds; so to prevent those vain, windy, frothy thoughts the heart naturally ingenders, and which arise from emptiness, first fill thy heart with the thoughts of God; *go down into his Wine-cellar, Cant. 2, 4*: observe it when you will, when you first open your eyes, there stand many suitors attending on you, to speak with your thoughts, even as clients at Lawyer's doors, many vanities and businesses; but speak thou with God first, he will say something to thy heart, will settle it for all day: and this do before the crowd of business comes in upon thee: of some Heathens it is said that they worship *that* as their *God*, for all day, which they first see in the morning; so it is with the idols of men's hearts.

Fifthly, have a watchful eye, and observe thy heart all day, though they crowd in, yet observe them, let them know that they

Ps. 5:3 My voice shalt thou hear in the morning, O LORD; in the morning will I direct my prayer unto thee, and will look up.
Ps. 143:8 Cause me to hear thy lovingkindness in the morning; for in thee do I trust: cause me to know the way wherein I should walk; for I lift up my soul unto thee.
Prov. 4:23 Keep thy heart with all diligence; for out of it are the issues of life.

pass not unseen; if a man would pray aright, he must watch also; where strict watch and ward is kept, and Magistrates observant who comes in, and who goes out, the Marshal and Constable diligent to examine vagrant persons, you shall have few there; that such swarms of vagrant thoughts make their rendezvous, and pass, is because there is not strict watch kept.

This is in a manner all thou canst do, for they will pass however, but yet complain thou of them, whip them, and give them their pass.

Sixthly, please not thy fancy too much with vanities and curious sights, this engenders vain thoughts; therefore *Job* says, *chap.* **xxxi.** *verse* 1, *that he made a covenant with his eyes, lest he should think upon a Maid, Proverbs* iv. 25, *let thine eyes look right on.*

Seventhly, be diligent in thy calling, and *whatsoever thine hand finds to do, do it with all thy might,* as it is, *Ecclesiastes* ix. 10, that is putting to, all the intention

Mt. 26:41 Watch and pray, that ye enter not into temptation: the spirit indeed is willing, but the flesh is weak.
Job 31:1 I made a covenant with mine eyes; why then should I think upon a maid?
Prov. 4:25 Let thine eyes look right on, and let thine eyelids look straight before thee.
Ecc. 9:10 Whatsoever thy hand findeth to do, do it with thy might; for there is no work, nor device, nor knowledge, nor wisdom, in the grave, whither thou goest.

_____

_____

_____

_____

_____

_____

_____

_____

_____

_____

_____

_____

_____

and strength of the mind that may be in it; let all the stream run to turn about thy Mill; the keeping thy thoughts to that channel, keeps them from overflowing into vanity and folly, 2 *Thessalonians* iii. 11, *those that labour not, are busy bodies;* and 1 *Timothy* v. 13, *idle, wandering,* περίεργοι, they are not only called ἀργοὶ, *Idle* only, because not busy about what they should, but περίεργοι, as intent on things they should not, they go from house to house: so their bodies do, because their minds do wander, having no centre. When *David* walked alone, what extravagancy did his spirit run into? let the ground lie fallow, and what weeds will there soon grow in it? God hath appointed us our callings to entertain our thoughts, and to find them work, and to hold them doing in the *interims*, between the duties of his worship, because the spirit and thoughts of men are restless, and will be busied some way; as therefore Kings keep those men that have active spirits in continual employment, lest their heads should be working

2 Thess. 3:11 For we hear that there are some which walk among you disorderly, working not at all, but are busybodies.

1 Tim. 5:13 And withal they learn to be idle, wandering about from house to house; and not only idle, but tattlers also and busybodies, speaking things which they ought not.

Prov. 31:27 She looketh well to the ways of her household, and eateth not the bread of idleness.

and plotting amiss: so did God appoint even in Paradise the active spirit of man, a calling, to keep him doing. God hereby hedgeth in man's thoughts, and sets them to go in a narrow lane, knowing that if they are unconfined and left at liberty, they would like wild *Asses snuff up the wind,* as *Jeremiah* speaks, *Jer.* ii. 24, only take heed of encumbering thy mind with too much business, more than thou canst grasp. It made *Martha* forget that *one thing necessary,* being *encumbered with many things, Luke* x. 40, this breeds care μέριμναι, which distracts the mind, (so the word signifies, ἀπὸ τῦ μερίζειν, as *dividing it*), and so causeth wandering thoughts, nothing more, so that the mind is not it self. For this weakens it, enervates it, and this being vanity, *Exodus* xviii. 18, said *Jethro* to *Moses,* when encumbered with business, *thou wilt fade away as a leaf,* out of which the moisture is dried up, even that juice which should be left for good duties will be exhausted, as dreams come through multitude of business, *Eccles.*

Gen. 2:15 And the LORD God took the man, and put him into the garden of Eden to dress it and to keep it.
Jer. 2:24 A wild ass used to the wilderness, that snuffeth up the wind at her pleasure; in her occasion who can turn her away? all they that seek her will not weary themselves; in her month they shall find her.
Lk. 10:40-42 But Martha was cumbered about much serving, and came to him, and said, Lord, dost thou not care that my sister hath left me to serve alone? bid her therefore that she help me. And Jesus answered and said unto her, Martha, Martha, thou art careful and troubled about many things: But one thing is needful: and Mary hath chosen that good part, which shall not be taken away from her.
Ex. 18:18 Thou wilt surely wear away, both thou, and this people that is with thee: for this thing is too heavy for thee; thou art not able to perform it thyself alone.

_____

_____

_____

_____

_____

_____

_____

_____

_____

_____

_____

_____

v. 3, so do a multitude of thoughts from a cumber of business.

Eighthly, in thy calling, and all thy works, for the success of thy ways therein, *commit thy ways to God, Proverbs* xvi. 3, *commit thy way unto the Lord, and thy thoughts shall be established, or ordered*: that is, kept from that confusion and disorder, and those swarms of cares, which others are annoyed with: and thereby thy aims may be as well accomplished: a few thoughts of faith would save us many thoughts of cares and fears, in the businesses we go about, which prove therefore *vain*, because they forward not at all the business we intend. When such waves toss the heart and turmoil it, and the winds of passions are up, if a few thoughts of faith come into the heart, they calm all presently.

FINIS.

28 MY 52

Ecc. 5:3 For a dream cometh through the multitude of business; and a fool's voice is known by multitude of words.
Prov. 16:3 Commit thy works unto the LORD, and thy thoughts shall be established.
Jam. 1:6 But let him ask in faith, nothing wavering. For he that wavereth is like a wave of the sea driven with the wind and tossed.
Is. 26:3 Thou wilt keep him in perfect peace, whose mind is stayed on thee: because he trusteth in thee.

*** THE Editor of this little work having made some considerable Collections towards an enlarged Biography of the Author, DR. THOMAS GOODWIN, would like to communicate with any one who may be in possession of authentic Anecdotes relating to his personal history, or Manuscripts bearing thereupon, or in short, whatever (apparently the most trivial) that could add to the stock of information respecting his life, character, and experience.

Contributions towards the above object would be very gratefully received and acknowledged. Address T. G. Post Office, Waltham Abbey, Essex ; or care of the Publisher, 45, Frith Street, Soho, London.

LATELY PUBLISHED.

THE SPIRITUAL USE OF AN ORCHARD OR GARDEN OF FRUIT TREES. Set forth in divers Similitudes between Natural and Spiritual Fruit Trees, according to Scripture and Experience. By RALPH AUSTEN, Practiser in the Art of Planting. Price 5s.

"Now learn a parable of the Fig Tree."—Matthew xxiv. 32 ; Mark xiii. 28.

Carefully re-printed from the 4to. Oxford Edition of 1657.

THE FOLLOWING ON SALE

AT THE

REDUCED PRICES AFFIXED.

A Selection from the works of that eminent servant of Christ, MR. JOHN BUNYAN, formerly Minister of the Gospel, and Pastor of a congregation at Bedford; consisting of thirteen Discourses, and his "Grace Abounding, &c." selected by the late REV. ISAAC BEEMAN : in three volumes—handsomely printed in large type by BENSLEY, in 1827—NOW REDUCED TO TWELVE SHILLINGS.

The Remains of the Rev. Isaac Beeman, late Minister of the Gospel at Providence Chapel, Cranbrook, Kent. Substance of Sermons and Letters, &c. in two volumes, with portrait,—handsomely printed in large type, 1844—Now Reduced to Twelve Shillings.

Some Account of the Life and Experience of George Payton, formerly Minister of the Gospel at Edenbridge, Kent. Second Edition, 1819, Now Reduced to Eighteen-Pence.

LONDON:

WILLIAM PAMPLIN, 45, FRITH STREET, SOHO.

LONDON:

PRINTED BY T. PETTITT, 1, OLD COMPTON STREET,

SOHO.

End of 1850 book.

Appendix

Appendix A – Original Title Page of the 1637 printing

Appendix B – Memoir of Thomas Goodwin, DD, by his son
From the 1890 book *The Works of Thomas Goodwin, Vol.2*

Appendix C – Epitaph on tomb at Bunhill Fields, London
From the 1890 book *The Works of Thomas Goodwin, Vol.2*

THE
VANITY
OF
THOVGHTS
DISCOVERED:

WITH
THEIR DANGER
AND CVRE.

BY
THO: GOODVVIN, *B.D.*

LONDON,
Printed by *M. F.* for *R. Dawlman,* and
L. Fawne, at the ſigne of the brazen
Serpent in *Pauls* Church-yard, 1637.

Appendix A: Original Title Page of the 1637 printing

MEMOIR OF THOMAS GOODWIN, D.D.

COMPOSED OUT OF HIS OWN PAPERS AND MEMOIRS, BY HIS SON.

THOMAS GOODWIN, the eldest son of Richard and Catherine Goodwin, the name of whose family was Collingwood, was born October 5, 1600, at Rollesby, a little village in Norfolk. He was brought up religiously by his parents, and they, devoting him to the ministry of the gospel, gave him also a learned education. After some time spent in school, having got the knowledge of the Latin and Greek tongues, he was sent to Cambridge, August 25, 1613, and placed in Christ's College, under the tuition and instruction of Mr William Power, one of the Fellows there. He continued about six years in that college, which flourished in a fulness of all exercises of learning, and in the number of scholars, there being two hundred of them : but, A.D. 1619, he left it, and removed to Catherine Hall, the state of which seemed so contemptible to him, there being no more than sixteen scholars, and few acts or exercises of learning had been performed for a long time, that though he was chosen Fellow, and also lecturer for the year 1620, yet he had some thoughts of leaving it again. He had, by an unwearied industry in his studies, so much improved those natural abilities which God had given him, that though so very young, he had gained a great esteem in the University. But all this time he walked in the vanity of his mind ; and ambitious designs and hopes entirely possessing him, all his aim was to get applause, to raise his reputation, and in any manner to advance himself by preferments. But God, who had destined him to higher ends than what he had projected in his own thoughts, was graciously pleased to change his heart, and to turn the course of his life to his own service and glory. But as the account of the work of the Holy Spirit on his soul will be most acceptable as related by himself, I shall present it in his own words :—

'Though by the course of nature in my first birth I was not like to live, being born before my time, and therefore of a weak constitution, yet God so

Appendix B: Memoir of Thomas Goodwin, DD, by his son

kept and strengthened me, that he preserved me, as David says, when I hung upon my mother's breasts; as one in whom he meant to manifest his grace, in the miraculous conversion of my soul unto himself. He did often stir up in me in my childish years the sparks of conscience, to keep me from gross sins, and to set me upon performing common duties. I began to have some slighter workings of the Spirit of God from the time I was six years old; I could weep for my sins whenever I did set myself to think of them, and had flashes of joy upon thoughts of the things of God. I was affected with good motions and affections of love to God and Christ, for their love revealed to man, and with grief for sin as displeasing them. This shewed how far good-ness of nature might go, as well in myself as others, to whom yet true sanctifying grace never comes. But this I thought was grace; for I reasoned within myself it was not by nature. I received the sacrament at Easter, when I was fourteen years old, and for that prepared myself as I was able. I set myself to examine whether I had grace or not; and by all the signs in Ursin's Catechism, which was in use among the Puritans in the College, I found them all, as I thought, in me. The love of God to such a sinner, and Christ's dying for me, did greatly affect me; and at that first sacrament I received, with what inward joy and comfort did I sing with the rest the 103d Psalm, which was usually sung during the administration! After having received it, I felt my heart cheered after a wonderful manner, thinking my-self sure of heaven, and judging all these workings to be infallible tokens of God's love to me, and of grace in me: all this while not considering that these were but more strong fits of nature's working. God hereby made way to advance the power of his grace the more in me, by shewing me how far I might go and yet deceive myself, and making me know that grace is a thing surpassing the power of nature; and therefore he suffered me to fall away, not from these good motions, for I could raise them when I would, but from the practice of them; insomuch as then my heart began to suspect them as counterfeit.

'I made a great preparation for the next ensuing sacrament at Whitsuntide, and in the meantime I went to hear Mr Sibbs, afterward Dr Sibbs, then lecturer at Trinity Church to the town of Cambridge, whose lectures the Puritans frequented. I also read Calvin's Institutions, and oh, how sweet was the reading of some parts of that book to me! How pleasing was the delivery of truths in a solid manner then to me! Before the sacrament was administered, I looked about upon the holy men in Christ's College, where I was bred; and how affected was I that I should go to heaven along with them! I particularly remember Mr Bently, a Fellow of that College, who was a dear child of God, and so died, and I then looked on him with joy, as one with whom I should live for ever in heaven.

'When I was in my place in the chapel, ready to receive the sacrament, being little of stature, the least in the whole University then, and for divers years, it fell out that my tutor, Mr Power, seeing me, sent to me that I should not receive it, but go out before all the College, which I did. This so much damped me, as I greatly pitied myself, but chiefly for this that my soul, which was full of expectation from this sacrament, was so unexpectedly disappointed of the opportunity. For I had long before verily thought that if I received that sacrament, I should be so confirmed that I should never fall away. But after this disappointment I left off praying, for being discouraged, I knew not how to go to God. I desisted from going to hear Dr Sibbs any more; I no more studied sound divinity, but gave myself to such studies as should enable me to preach after the mode, then of high applause in the University, which Dr Senhouse brought up, and was applauded above all by the scholars.

'It now fell out that Arminianism was set afoot in Holland, and the rest of those Provinces, and it continued hottest at that very time when I was thus wrought upon. I perceived by their doctrine, which I understood, being inquisitive, that they acknowledged a work of the Spirit of God to begin with men, by moving and stirring the soul; but free-will then from its freedom carried it, though assisted by those aids and helps. And this work of the Spirit they called grace, sufficient in the first beginnings of it, exciting, moving, and helping the will of man to turn to God, and giving him power to turn, when being thus helped he would set himself to do it: but withal they affirmed, that though men are thus converted, yet by the freedom of the same will they may, and do, often in time fall away totally; and then upon another fit through the liberty of the will, again assisted with the like former helps, they return again to repentance. Furthermore, I am yet to tell you how I was withal acquainted during this season with several holy youths in Christ's College, who had made known unto me the workings of God upon them, in humiliation, faith, and change of heart. And I observed that they continued their profession steadfast, and fell not off again.

'Though the Arminian doctrines suited my own experience, in these natural workings of conscience off and on in religion, yet the example of those godly youths in their constant perseverance therein made so strong an impression upon me, that in my very heart and judgment I thought the doctrine of Arminianism was not true; and I was fixed under a conviction that my state was neither right nor sound; but yet I could not imagine wherein it failed and was defective. But notwithstanding my falling thus away, yet I still upon every sacrament set myself anew to examine myself, to repent, and to turn to God; but when the sacrament was over, I returned to a neglect of praying, and to my former ways of unregenerate principles and practices, and to live in hardness of heart and profaneness. When I was thus given over to the strength of my lusts, and further off from all goodness than ever I had been, and utterly out of hope that God would ever be so good unto me as to convert me; and being resolved to follow the world, and the glory, applause, preferment, and honour of it, and to use all means possible for these attainments; when I was one day going to be merry with my companions at Christ's College, from which I had removed to Catherine Hall, by the way hearing a bell toll at St Edmund's for a funeral, one of my company said there was a sermon, and pressed me to hear it. I was loath to go in, for I loved not preaching, especially not that kind of it which good men used, and which I thought to be dull stuff. But yet, seeing many scholars going in, I thought it was some eminent man, or if it were not so, that I would come out again.

'I went in before the hearse came, and took a seat ; and fain would I have been gone, but shame made me stay. I was never so loath to hear a sermon in my life. Inquiring who preached, they told me it was Dr Bambridge, which made me the more willing to stay, because he was a witty man. He preached a sermon which I had heard once before, on that text in Luke xix. 41, 42. I remember the first words of the sermon pleased me so well as to make me very attentive all the while. He spake of deferring repentance, and of the danger of doing so. Then he said that every man had his day, it was "this thy day," not to-morrow, but to-day. He shewed also that every man had a time in which grace was offered him ; and if he neglected it, it was just with God that it should be hidden from his eyes. And that as, in things temporal, it was an old saying that every man had an opportunity, which if he took hold of he was made for ever ; so in spirituals, every man hath a time, in which, if he would know the things which belong unto his peace, he was made for ever, but otherwise they would be hid from his eyes. This a little moved me, as I had wont to be at other sermons. Then he came to shew that the neglect of this had final impenitency, blindness of mind, and hardness of heart ; concluding with this saying, " Every day thou prayest, pray to God to keep thee from blindness of mind, and hardness of heart."

'The matter of the sermon was vehemently urged on the hearer, (whoever he was that deferred his repentance,) not to let slip the opportunity of that day, but immediately to turn to God and defer no longer ; being edged with that direful threatening, lest if he did not turn to God in that day, the day of grace and salvation, it might be eternally hid from his eyes. I was so far affected, as I uttered this speech to a companion of mine that came to church with me, and indeed that brought me to that sermon, that I hoped to be the better for this sermon as long as I lived. I and that companion of mine had come out of our own chambers at Catherine Hall, with a fixed design to have gone to some of my like acquaintance at Christ's College, where I had been bred, on purpose to be merry and spend that afternoon ; but as I went along, was accidentally persuaded to hear some of the sermon. This was on Monday the 2d of October 1620, in the afternoon. As soon as we came out of the church, I left my fellows to go on to Christ's College ; but my thoughts being retired then, I went to Catherine Hall, and left all my acquaintance, though they sent after me to come.

'I thought myself to be as one struck down by a mighty power. The grosser sins of my conversation came in upon me, which I wondered at, as being unseasonable at first ; and so the working began, but was prosecuted still more and more, higher and higher : and I endeavouring not to think the least thought of my sins, was passively held under the remembrance of them, and affected, so as I was rather passive all the while in it than active, and my thoughts held under, whilst that work went on.

'I remember some two years after, I preaching at Ely in the minster, as they call it, in a turn of preaching for Dr Hills, prebend of that church, Master of our College; I told the auditory, meaning myself in the person of another, that a man to be converted, who is ordinarily ignorant of what the work of conversion should be, and what particular passages it consists of, was yet guided through all the dark corners and windings of it, as would be a wonder to think of, and would be as if a man were to go to the top of that lantern, to bring him into all the passages of the minster, within doors and without, and knew not a jot of the way, and were in every step in danger to tread awry and fall down. So it was with me; I knew no more of that work of conversion than these two general heads, that a man was troubled in conscience for his sins, and afterwards was comforted by the favour of God manifested to him. And it became one evidence of the truth of the work of grace upon me, when I reviewed it, that I had been so strangely guided in the dark. In all this intercourse, and those that follow to the very end, I was acted all along by the Spirit of God being upon me, and my thoughts passively held fixed, until each head and sort of thoughts were finished, and then a new thought began and continued; that I have looked at them as so many conferences God had with me by way of reproof and conviction. My thoughts were kept fixed and intent on the consideration of the next immediate causes of those fore-gone gross acts of sinning. An abundant discovery was made unto me of my inward lusts and concupiscence, and how all sorts of concupiscences had wrought in me; at which I was amazed, to see with what greediness I had sought the satisfaction of every lust.

'Indeed, natural conscience will readily discover grosser acts against knowledge; as in the dark a man more readily sees chairs and tables in a room, than flies and motes: but the light which Christ now vouchsafed me, and this new sort of illumination, gave discovery of my heart in all my sin-nings, carried me down to see the inwards of my belly, as Solomon speaks, and searched the lower rooms of my heart, as it were with candles, as the prophet's phrase is. I saw the violent eagerness, unsatiableness of my lusts; and moreover concerning the dispensation of God in this new light, I found the apparent difference, by experience of what I had received in former times. I had before had enlightenings and great stirrings of the Holy Ghost, both unto and in the performance of holy duties, prayer, and hearing, and the like; and yet I had not the sinful inordinacy of my lusts discovered, which had been the root and ground of all my other sinnings. And these forementioned devotions were different also in this respect from the present sight of my inward corruptions, that in all the former, though I felt myself much stirred, yet I had this secret thought run along, that God could not but accept those real services which I thought I did perform; and so I fell into the opinion of merit, which thought I could not get rid of, though the common received doctrine taught me otherwise. But now when I saw my lusts and heart in that clear manner as I did, God quitted me of that opi-nion, which vanished without any dispute, and I detested myself for my former thoughts of it. And the sinfulness of these lusts I saw chiefly to lie in ungodliness as the spring of them; forasmuch as I had been a lover of pleasure more than a lover of God: according to that in Jeremiah, "My people have committed two evils: they have forsaken me the fountain of living waters, and have made unto themselves cisterns that will hold no water." And these lusts I discerned to have been acted by me in things that were most lawful, answerably unto that saying in Scripture, "The very ploughing of the wicked is sin:" and by the clear light thereof, the sinfulness of my sin was exceedingly enlarged; for that light accompanied me through all and every action that I could cast my remembrance upon, or that my view went over.

'And by and through the means of the discovery of those lusts, a new horrid vein and course of sin was revealed also to me, that I saw lay at the bottom of my heart, in the rising and working of all my lusts; namely, that they kept my heart in a continual course of ungodliness,—that is, that my heart was wholly obstructed from acting towards God any way, or from having any holy or good movings at all.

'God having proceeded thus far, I perceived I was "humbled under his mighty hand," as James speaks, with whom only and immediately I had to do, and not with my own bare single thoughts. But God continued orderly to possess my thoughts with a further progress as to this subject; I being made sensible of God's hand in it, and myself was merely passive: but still God continued his hand over me, and held me, intent to consider and pierce into what should be the first causes of so much actual sinfulness; and he presented to me, as in answer thereunto,—for it was transacted as a conference by God with me,—the original corruption of my nature, and inward evil constitution and depravation of all my faculties; the inclinations and disposednesses of heart unto all evil, and averseness from all spiritual good and acceptableness unto God. I was convinced that in this respect I was flesh, which was to my apprehension as if that had been the definition of a man, "that which is born of the flesh is flesh."

'And here let me stand a while astonished, as I did then: I can compare this sight, and the workings of my heart rising from thence, to be as if I had in the heat of summer looked down into the filth of a dungeon, where by a clear light and piercing eye I discerned millions of crawling living things in the midst of that sink and liquid corruption. Holy Mr Price's comparison was, that when he heard Mr Chattertom preach the gospel, his apprehension was as if the sun, namely Jesus Christ, shined upon a dunghill; but my sight of my heart was, to my sense, that it was utterly without Christ. How much and deeply did I consider that all the sins that ever were committed by the wickedest men that have been in the world had proceeded from the corruption of their nature; or that the sins which any or all men did commit at any time were from the same root; and I by my nature, if God had left me and withdrawn from me, should have committed the same, as any temptation should have induced me unto the like. But what much affected me was a sight and sense that my heart was empty of all good; that in me, that is, in my flesh, there dwelt no good, not a mite of truly spiritual good, as the Scripture describes true inherent grace to be some good in us toward the Lord our God, which none of my goodness nor ingenuity was, which I boasted of. What is all such goodness to God who is only good, and is the only true measure of all that is called good? which is so only so far as it respects him, as he is holy and good, as of the law it is said, Rom. vii. Thus at present I was abundantly convinced.

'But next I was brought to inquire into and consider of what should have been the original cause at the bottom of all this forementioned sinfulness, both in my heart and life. And after I had well debated with myself that one place, Rom. v. 12, "By one man sin entered into the world, and death by him, and passed upon all men, in whom," or in that, "all have sinned:" that it was in him they all sinned, for they had not in and of themselves sinned actually, as those that die infants, "after the similitude of Adam's transgression;" which limitation is cautiously there added by the Apostle, to shew that they had not actually sinned of themselves, but are simply involved in his act of sinning; and that sin wherein we were all involved, as guilty of it, is expressly said to be the disobedience of that one man; for by one man's disobedience, many of his children of the sons of men were all made sinners, for disobedience notes an act of sinning, not a sinful nature or a habit. This caused me necessarily to conceive thus of it, that it was the guilt or demerit of that one man's disobedience that corrupted my nature. Under such like apprehensions as these did my spirit lie convicted so strongly of this great truth, that being gone to bed some hours before, and filled with these meditations, I in the end of all rose out of bed, being alone, and solemnly fell down on my knees before God, the Father of all the family in heaven, and did on my own accord assume and take on me the guilt of that sin, as truly as any of my own actual sins. But now when I was thus concluding in my own heart concerning my sinfulness, that all that I had acted was wholly corrupt, and that in me there was nothing but flesh, as born of flesh, so that all the actions that came from me were wholly corrupt, and in me, that is in my flesh, there dwelt no good thing, Rom. vii., my pronouncing this conclusion with myself was presently interrupted by the remembrance, which not till now did come in full upon me, in this nick of time and not before.

'The interruption was made by these intervening thoughts, that I had forgot myself, and should wrong myself to end in this conclusion; for I had had abundance of experience, as I thought, of the workings of true grace, enlightenings and ravishments of spirit and of faith in Christ, at sacrament and at other times. I recalled the course of my spirit until I was towards thirteen years old, for I was not thirteen when I came to the University; and I recalled to my remembrance, that during that space when I was seven years old, my grandfather, whom I lived with, had a servant, who observing some sin in me, reproved me sharply, and laid open hell-torments as due to me, whither, he said, I must go for such sins, and was very vehement with me; and I was accordingly affected with thoughts of God and matters of religion from thenceforth. I was indeed but in my infancy, in respect of my knowledge of religion, having childish thoughts, which I began to build my hopes on. For my conscience was opened with the sight of my sins when I committed any, and from that time I began to weep and mourn for my sins, and for a while to forbear to commit them, but found I was weak, and was overcome again; but I could weep for my sins when I could weep for nothing: and I doing this privately between God and myself, concluded it was not hypocrisy. I thought of Hezekiah's example, who turned to the wall and wept, and how it moved God; for I was brought up to read the Scriptures from a child, and I met with that promise of our Saviour's, "Whatever you shall ask the Father in my name, I will do it for you:" and that made me confident, for to be sure I would use his name for whatever I would have of God. Yet still I fell into sins, renewing my repentance for them. As Paul says, when I was a child, my thoughts were as a child, and I judged that whatever is more than nature must be grace; and when I had my affections any way exercised upon the things of the other world, thought I, This is the work of God, for the time was I had no such actings.

'And thus my younger time was at times spent; but God was to me as a wayfaring man, who came and dwelt for a night, and made me religious for a fit, but then departed from me. The Holy Ghost moved upon the waters when the world was creating, and held and sustained the chaos that was created, and so he does in carnal men's hearts; witness their good motions at times. In a great frost, you shall see, where the sun shines hot, the ice drops, and the snow melts, and the earth grows slabby; but it is a particular thaw only where the sun shines, not a general thaw of all things that are frozen. But so it was, that for these lighter impressions and slighter workings, my heart did grow so presumptuous, that I thought myself not only to have grace, but more grace than my relations, or any inhabitant of the town that I knew of, and this for the time I was a schoolboy before I came to the University.

'When I was past twelve years old, towards thirteen, I was admitted into Christ's College in Cambridge, as a junior sophister, a year before the usual time of standing; and there being the opportunity of a sacrament of the Lord's Supper, appointed to be administered publicly in the College, and all of that form that I was now in being taken into receiving, I was ashamed to go out of the chapel alone and not receive, and so I adventured to obtrude myself upon that ordinance with the rest. I had set myself to the greatest preparation I could possibly make, in repenting of my sins and examining myself, and by meditations on the sufferings of Christ, which I presumed to apply to myself, with much thankfulness to God. And that which now, since I came to that College, had quickened and heightened my devotion, was, that there remained still in the College six Fellows that were great tutors, who professed religion after the strictest sort, then called Puritans. Besides, the town was then filled with the discourse of the power of Mr Perkins' ministry, still fresh in most men's memories; and Dr Ames, that worthy professor of divinity at Franeker, who wrote *Puritanismus Anglicanus*, had been Fellow

of that College, and not long before my time had, by the urgency of the
Master, been driven both from the College and University. The worth and
holiness of that man are sufficiently known by what he did afterwards in the
Low Countries. These Puritan Fellows of that College had several pupils
that were godly, and I fell into the observation of them and their ways. I
had also the advantage of Ursin's Catechism, which book was the renowned
summaries of the orthodox religion, and the Puritan Fellows of the College
explained it to their pupils on Saturday night, with chamber prayers. This
book I was upon this occasion acquainted with; and against the time of the
forementioned sacrament, I examined myself by it, and I found, as I thought,
all things in that book and my own heart to agree for my preparation.

'As I grew up, the noise of the Arminian controversy in Holland, at the
Synod of Dort, and the several opinions of that controversy, began to be
every man's talk and inquiry, and possessed my ears. That which I
observed, as touching the matter of my own religion, was, that those godly
Fellows, and the younger sort of their pupils that were godly, held constantly
to their strict religious practices and principles, without falling away and
declining, as I knew of. I judged them to be in the right for matter of
religion, and the Arminians in the wrong, who held falling away; yea, and
I did so far reverence the opinions of the orthodox, who are against the
power of free-will, and for the power of electing grace, that I did so far judge
myself as to suspect I had not grace because of my so often falling away;
whereof I knew not any probabler reason that it was not true grace which I
had built upon, than this, that still after sacraments I fell away into neglects
of duties and into a sinful course, which those godly youths I had in my eye
did not.

'But that which chiefly did serve most to convince me, was the powerful
and steady example of one of those godly Fellows in the College, Mr Bently,
who was a man of an innocent, meek, humble spirit and demeanour, and an
eminent professor of religion in the greatest strictness, whose profession was
further quickened and enhanced by this, that he lived in a continual fear of
death, having had two fits of an apoplexy that laid him for dead, and daily
expecting a third. This blessed man I observed and reverenced above all
other men but Mr Price, who then was of the University, an eminent example
of conversion in the eyes of all, and who was afterwards minister of the
gospel in Lynn Regis. I remember that when I came to the prayers, I
used to have usually great stirrings of affections and of my bodily spirits to
a kind of ravishment, and so I continued in private devotion for a week
after; yet still all those impressions proved to be but morning dew, and
came to nothing, and I utterly forbore to pray privately, or exercise any
other good duty, and so all my religion was soon lost and came to nothing.
But again, when the time of the next sacrament came, I renewed the former
exercises, and then I grew into a love of the good scholars of the College, both
of Fellows and others, and began to continue more constant in duties for a
longer time together.

'And I left going to St Mary's, the university church, where were all the

florid sermons and strains of wit in which that age abounded, the great wits
of those times striving who of them should exceed each other. But from
these the work I had the next sacrament upon me did so far withdraw me,
as for eight weeks together I went with the Puritans of that College to hear
Dr Sibbs, whose preaching was plain and wholesome; and to improve my
time the better before sermon began, I carried with me Calvin's Institutions to church, and found a great deal of sweetness and savouriness in that
divinity. In those weeks I kept constantly to private prayer, and calling to
mind the sweetness of this course, of those eight weeks in these exercises,
and acquainting myself more with the youths of that College who held
steadfast in their profession. Oh, how did I long for the receiving of the
next sacrament, in which I hoped the body and blood of Christ received
with due preparation, which I endeavoured to make to the utmost of my
ability, would confirm me in the way I had begun and continued in so long,
and would strengthen me for ever from falling into the same way of liking
florid and scholastic sermons.

'I went to chapel for the sacrament, as I was wont to do, and expected
no other but to receive it; but in the nick, when every communicant was
rising to go to kneel at the step, as the manner was, my tutor, Mr Power,
(who was the only tutor that ever I had,) sent a messenger to me to command me out of the chapel, and to forbear to receive; which message I
received with extreme dolour of heart and trouble; but he being my tutor,
I obeyed him. But upon this disappointment I was so discouraged, that I
left off private prayer for the first week after, and at last altogether, and
from thence after went constantly to St Mary's, where the flaunting sermons
were; and though I never fell into the common sins of drunkenness or
whoredom, whereunto I had temptations and opportunities enough, yet I
returned unto the lusts and pleasures of sinning, but especially the ambition
of glory and praise, prosecuting those lusts with the whole of my soul. And
though I did not walk in profane ways against religion, yet with a lower
kind of enmity against good men and good things, resolving to have preached
against those at Lynn and their ways, and to have taken part with the
whole town against them; which my wicked spirit was too eager and fitted
to do by the studies I had pursued; it came to this at last, that if God
would give me the pleasure I desired, and the credit and preferment I pursued after, and not damn me at last, let him keep heaven to himself; and I
often thought thus with myself, They talk of their Puritan powerful preaching, and of Mr Rogers of Dedham, and such others, but I would gladly see
the man that could trouble my conscience.

'When God now by a true work of grace effectually converted me to himself, the vanity of my former religion was, by serious reflections on these
passages mentioned, sufficiently manifested. The deficiency of the root of
all my devotions did also abundantly add to the discovery. For God did
vouchsafe me a new and further light into the bottom of my heart, to
discern that self-love and self-flattery, acted by the motives of the word so
far as they will extend, were but the roots of all these gaudy tulips which I

counted grace : and I needed no other scripture than that in the parable, together with my own heart, for the proof of it : Mark iv. 5, 6, "Some fell upon stony ground, where it had not much earth ; and immediately it sprang up, because it had no depth of earth : but when the sun was up, it was scorched ; and because it had no root, it withered away." And with this one blast, and thus easily, did the flower of all my former devotions wither and come to nought, because they wanted moisture in the heart to nourish them.

'By the prospect of all these heads of sinning which I lay under, I was surrounded and shut up, and saw no way to escape : but together with the sight of all this sinfulness, hell opened his mouth upon me, threatening to devour and destroy me ; and I began withal to consider the eternity of time that I was to pass through under this estate, that it was for ever and ever. But though I was subjugated and bound over to these apprehensions, yet God kept me from the soreness of his wrath, and its piercing my soul through and through : that though I had a solid and strong conviction of God's wrath abiding on me, as being in a state of unbelief, yet my soul suffered not the terrors of the Almighty, though I lay bound as it were hand and foot, subacted under the pressure of the guilt of wrath, or of being subject to the just judgment of the Lord, as the word is to be translated, Rom. iii. 19. How long my soul lay filled with these thoughts, I perfectly remember not ; but it was not many hours before God, who after we are regenerate is so faithful and mindful of his word, and his word of promise, as to suffer us not to be tempted above what we are able, but will with the temptation also make a way to escape, that we may be able to bear it ; and he loving us with the same love as we are his own dear elect, does not often suffer a destroying apprehension to continue long upon us, but out of the same faithfulness and pity to us finds a way to escape.

I do not speak now of temptations, but of the just conviction which many such souls have, previous unto their believing. See what God says, Ezek. xvi., of the whole body of his elect church, comparing their condition to that of a child born dead, and covered over with blood, as it came out of the womb, the navel not cut, neither washed in water, but in this plight cast out into the open field, as a child that was dead, among the carcases. And therefore God, when he was said to have compassion on him, said to him, Live, which implies that he was dead. In this plight was my soul, dead in sins and trespasses from my nativity, and from thence so continuing to that very day, together with that heap of actual sins, that were the continual ebullitions of original sin. And no eye pitied me or could help me, but as God there, in Ezek. xvi., on the sudden,—for it is spoken as a speedy word, as well as a vehement earnest word, for it is doubled twice, 'yea, I said unto you, Live,'—so God was pleased on the sudden, and as it were in an instant, to alter the whole of his former dispensation towards me, and said of and to my soul, Yea, live ; yea, live, I say, said God : and as he created the world and the matter of all things by a word, so he created and put a new life and spirit into my soul, and so great an alteration was strange to me.

'The word of promise which he let fall into my heart, and which was but as it were softly whispered to my soul; and as when a man speaks afar off, he gives a still, yet a certain sound, or as one hath expressed the preachings of the gospel by the apostles, that God whispered the gospel out of Zion, but the sound thereof went forth over the whole earth: so this speaking of God to my soul, although it was but a gentle sound, yet it made a noise over my whole heart, and filled and possessed all the faculties of my whole soul. God took me aside, and as it were privately said unto me, Do you now turn to me, and I will pardon all your sins though never so many, as I forgave and pardoned my servant Paul, and convert you unto me, as I did Mr Price, who was the most famous convert and example of religion in Cambridge. Of these two secret whispers and speeches of God to me, I about a year after did expressly tell Mr Price, in declaring to him this my conversion, while it was fresh with me, as he well remembered long; and I have since repeated them to others I know not how often, for they have ever stuck in my mind. And examples laid before us by God do give us hope, and are written and proposed unto us: Rom. xv. 4, "For whatsoever things were written to us aforetime were written for our learning, that we through patience and comfort of the Scriptures might have hope;" and we use to allege examples, not only to illustrate and explain rules, but to prove and confirm them. That God pardoned such a man in such a condition, is often brought home unto another man in the same condition, and impliedly contains a secret promise, that so he may do to me, says the soul in the same condition. And I remember that I, preaching at Ely two years after, urged to the people the example of Paul (which I was before referred to) as an example to win others, in having in my eye and thoughts the said experience of God's dealing with me in the same kind; and that the examples of such are to be held forth by God, as flags of mercy before a company of rebels to win them in.

'Now as to this example of Paul, it was full and pertinent for that purpose for which God held it out to me; I then considered with myself the amplitude of my pardon, that it involved all sorts of sins of the highest nature, in which Paul had so walked as he was even upon the narrow brink of sinning against the Holy Ghost. And God suggested unto me that he would pardon me all my sins, though never so great, for boldness, hardness of heart, and heinousness of sinning, as he had pardoned Paul, whose story of forgiveness I was referred unto; and also that he would change my heart, as he had done Mr Price's, who was in all men's eyes the greatest and most famous convert, known to the whole University of Cambridge, and made the greatest and notedest example that ever was, of a strange conversion to God, and who was the holiest man that ever I knew one or other, and was then preacher at King's Lynn, whither my parents had removed from Rollesby, and then lived there.

'The confirmations which myself have had, to judge that these instructions and suggestions were immediately from God, were these:—

'1. I considered the posture and condition of my spirit, and that this suggestion took me when my heart was fixed, and that unmoveably, in the contrary persuasions, not only that I was guilty of those sins, and had continued in them to that time, but that I was in a damned estate, without hope for remedy: and when God had set a guard upon me as the prisoner of hell, then came in these contrary apprehensions and impressions as it were in an instant; which impressions also were so deep and rooted in my heart, that I remembered them ever since. And I did accordingly acquaint Mr Price at Lynn, a year and a half after this, setting them on upon my heart, in rehearsing to him the story of my conversion, which he exceedingly approved of.

'2. It was a word in its proper season, like that which was spoken to Abraham, the father of all the faithful, and which ran in a proverb among the Jews: 'In the mount the Lord will be seen,' or 'provide;' which they apply to the immediate remedy which God does use to afford out of pity to a man in a strait or distress, and which none but himself can give remedy to. It is a word fitted and proper to such an occasion, and peculiar to the case of the person; a word that was quick and sudden, and interrupting all contrary expectations and fears, as the manner of the speech was, 'Abraham, Abraham,' as a man that speaks in haste to prevent any contrary fears. It is a word spoken in season, which Christ himself was taught by God to speak to distressed souls, Isa. l. 4.

'3. This that was suggested to me was not an ungrounded fancy, but the pure word of God, which is the ground of faith and hope. It was the promise and performance of God's forgiving of Paul the most heinous sins that ever any convert committed who was saved; for he was the chiefest of sinners, as himself confesses. And this instance was directed unto me, as the most pertinent to my case that I could elsewhere have found in the Book of God.

'4. In considering the consequents and effects that followed after God's speaking to me, I was hopefully persuaded it was from God, for the things were fulfilled which God had spoken of. For, first, I felt my soul, and all the powers of it, as in an instant, to be clean altered and changed in the dispositions of them; even as our own divines of Great Britain do set out in their discourse of the manner of conversion in the effect of it. Secondly, I found from the same time the works of the devil to be dissolved in my heart in an eminent manner, my understanding enlightened, my will melted and softened, and of a stone made flesh, disposed to receive, and disposed to turn to God. And, thirdly, I found my spirit clothed with a new nature, naturally inclining me to good; whereas before it was inclined only to evil. I found not only good motions from the Spirit of God, as he was pleased to incite me formerly, not only flushings and streamings of affection, which soon vanish, or stirring my bodily spirits with joy, when I applied myself to a holy duty, but I found a new indweller, or habitual principle of opposition to, and hatred of sin indwelling, so as I concluded with myself that this new workmanship wrought in me was of the same kind as to matter of holiness with that image of God expressed, Eph. iv. 23, 24, but more expressly

affirmed, Col. iii. 10.   It was this one disposition that at first comforted me,
that I saw and found two contrary principles, of spirit against flesh, and
flesh against spirit : and I found apparently the difference of the opposition
that only conscience makes against a lust, and that which the spirit—that is,
the new work of grace in a man's heart—makes against the flesh.   That the
spirit not only contradicted and checked, but made a real natural opposition,
such as fire does to water ; so that the spirit did as truly lust against the
work of the flesh, as the flesh against that of the spirit.   And this difference
I found not by reading, or hearing any one speak of it, but, as Austin did, I
perceived it of myself, and wondered at it ; for I may say of this combat,
that it is proper and peculiar to a man that is regenerate.   It is not in God
or Christ, who are a fulness of holiness ; not in devils, for they are all sin ;
not in good angels, for they are entirely holy ; not in wicked men, for they
have no grace in them, to fight with their corruptions after such a manner.
Fourthly, The consequent of this that fell out in my heart was an actual
turning from all known sins, and my entertaining the truth of all godliness,
and the principles of it, as far as I received it from the word of God, and
the best examples of godly men I lived withal.   And in general, I took this
course through God's direction and assistance, that I looked back upon my
sinful estate, and took a summary survey of my chiefest sins and lusts ; and I
found them to be love of pleasure more than of God, corrupt ends, especially
of vain-glory and academic praise, which I sought with my whole soul : and
God was pleased to direct me to take up, as the rule of my turning to him,
a sincere aim at his glory as the rule of all my inward thoughts, words,
actions, desires, and ends whatsoever.   And in this it pleased God to direct
and assist me, to consider asunder all the sorts of actions I had gone through
in my life, and to take them asunder in particulars, every one in order, but
especially the principallest of them.

'And here, in the first place, I considered what was the aim and drift of
my studies, which I had spent my whole time upon : and having been de-
voted by my parents for the work of the ministry, I considered what it was
did serve most to the glory of God in the work of the ministry, and that
overturned all the projects and designs of my heart hitherto, which were the
dearest of all to me ; so dear, that I would certainly rather not have lived,
than have forsaken that interest.   The University in those times was addicted
in their preaching to a vain-glorious eloquence, wherein the wits did strive
to exceed one another ; and that which I most of all affected, in my foolish
fancy, was to have preached, for the matter thereof, in the way that Dr Senhouse of St John's, afterwards made bishop, did exceed all men in.   I instance
in him, to explain the way and model that I set up, because his sermons,
five or six of them, are in print, and because it is the eminentest farrago
of all sorts of flowers of wit that are found in any of the fathers, poets, his-
tories, similitudes, or whatever has the elegancy of wit in it ; and in the
joining and disposing of these together, wit was the eminent orderer in a
promiscuous way.   His way I took for my pattern, not that I hoped to
attain to the same perfection, I coming far behind-hand of all the accom-

plishments he abounded in. But I set him up in my thoughts to imitate as much as I was able; and about such collections as these did I set my studies until I should come to preach.

'But this way of his did soon receive a fatal wound, Dr Preston opposing it, and preaching against it, as vain and unedifying. His catechetical sermons in the chapel of that College it fell out I heard whilst unregenerate; but they moved me not to alter my studies, nor should all the world have persuaded me to have done it, nor all angels, nor men; but my heart, upon this my turning to God and setting his glory as my resolved end of all my actions and ways, did soon discover to me the unprofitableness of such a design; and I came to this resolved principle, that I would preach wholly and altogether sound, wholesome words, without affectation of wit and vanity of eloquence. And in the end, this project of wit and vain-glory was wholly sunk in my heart, and I left all, and have continued in that purpose and practice these threescore years; and I never was so much as tempted to put in any of my own withered flowers that I had gathered, and valued more than diamonds, nor have they offered themselves to my memory to the bringing them into a sermon to this day, but I have preached what I thought was truly edifying, either for conversion of souls, or bringing them up to eternal life: so as I am free to profess that great maxim of Dr Preston, in his sermon of humiliation, on the first of the Ephesians, "that of all other, my master-lust was mortified."

'I observed of this work of God on my soul, that there was nothing of constraint or force in it, but I was carried on with the most ready and willing mind, and what I did was what I chose to do. With the greatest freedom I parted with my sins, formerly as dear to me as the apple of my eye, yea, as my life, and resolved never to return to them more. And what I did was from deliberate choice; I considered what I was doing, and reckoned with myself what it would cost me to make this great alteration. I considered the common opinion the world had of those ways of purity and holiness, and walked according to them. But though I considered what the common course and vogue of the world was concerning the ways of one that would be a true convert and sincere to God, yet they hindered me not at all. The weeds that entangled me in those waters, I swam and broke through, with as much ease as Samson did his withes; for I was made a vassal and a perfect captive to another binding, such as Paul speaks of, when he says he went bound in the Spirit to Jerusalem; and I said within myself, of all my old companions, What do you breaking my heart? I am not ready to be bound only, but to give up my life, so as I may serve God with joy in these ways. I parted with all my lusts, not as Lot's wife, looking back on what I departed from; but with my whole soul and whole desires, not to return more to the enjoyment of any lust, and casting down all those childish imaginations of preferment, such as scholars do generally aim at and promise to themselves, and to attain which they make their aim, and the card of their life they sail by. All these fell, and like bubbles broke and vanished to air; and those which I counted my strongest holds and imaginations, "and everything that exalteth itself, was brought into captivity and obedience to Christ," 2 Cor. x. 5. And I was brought in my own thoughts to be content with the meanest condition all my days, so as I might fulfil the course of my life, though never so mean, with uprightness and sincerity towards God.

'I took my leave for my whole life of all ecclesiastical preferments; and though afterwards I was President of Magdalene College, my great motive to it, from the bottom of my heart, was the fair opportunity of doing good in my ministry in the University, and that it might be in my power to bring in young men that were godly, both Fellows and students, that should serve God in the ministry in after-times. And after such as were godly did I inquire and seek, and valued such when I found them as the greatest jewels. And when I failed of such, it was a great affliction to me; but this was my heart and endeavour, as my own soul and conscience bears me witness, though I did and might fall short of this my own aim in some particular persons. And this principle I brought with me from Catherine Hall in Cambridge, where I had my first station, and where I was the instrument of the choice of that holy and reverend man, Dr Sibbs, to be Master of that College, and of most of the Fellows of that College in those times, as Dr Arrowsmith, and Mr Pen of Northamptonshire, to name no more. And I was the more fixedly established in the practice of this, that after I had been seven years from Cambridge, coming out of Holland, I had for some years after, well-nigh every month, serious and hearty acknowledgment from several young men, who had received the light of their conversion by my ministry while I was in the University of Cambridge. And this was the great encouragement I had to return again to a university, having enjoyed so frequent a testimony of the fruit of my labours while I was preacher at Cambridge; and what the success has been at Oxford, I leave to Christ till the latter day.

'But the most eminent property of my conversion to God, I have been speaking of, was this, that the glory of the great God was set up in my heart as the square and rule of each and every particular practice, both of faith and godliness, that I turned unto ; and of all signs of sincerity, there is, nor can be, none clearer than this, witness our Saviour Christ's speech, John vii. 18, "He that seeketh his glory that sent him, the same is true, and no unrighteousness is in him." Christ speaketh it of himself, who is the truth itself, and speaketh of himself out of his own experience of what he did who is the truth itself; and the glory of God is God himself, who doth all things for himself: and therefore he that acteth thus predominantly for God above all other ends, must necessarily be judged truly righteous. Nor can any man extract that out of his heart which is not in it. Now there is not the least spark of the glory of God in the heart of man unregenerate, and therefore cannot be extracted out of it, no, not the least spark. Take a flint, and strike it against steel or iron, and you shall have sparks struck out ; but if you take a piece of ice never so great, and strike it against a stone, or any other material, you shall not have a spark, for there is none in it, nor any disposition towards it. I remember that when I heard Dr Preston describing true spiritual change of heart, (it was upon Rom. xii. 2, "Be ye transformed by the renewing of your minds,") he spoke in this manner. "It is," said he, "when upon the change of a man's utmost end, there is a change made upon the whole man, and all the powers of his soul;" which when I had duly considered, I judged I never had anything more punctual, remembering this work of God upon myself at first. For, as he then discoursed it, "if a man changes but unto one particular end, and has but one particular and limited end, the effect is answerable, it is but partial so far as that end serves to: as if a man that had a humour of prodigality, and now thinks it concerns him to be sparing and covetous, this change of his end being but particular, has but a narrowed effect, namely as to sparing and care to keep his money, not to spend it lavishly; but godliness, the height of which lies in a respect to God and his glory above all things else, hath a general, yea, universal end, which extends its influence upon all things."

'Hence my task, from this principle, proved to be to survey and go over every particular kind of act, both what I must forbear, and for what end, and with what heart, as also to observe each particular practice of godliness, which I wretchedly had altogether for a long while lived in neglect of; and hereabout I began with what I was to forbear and practise no longer, but alter my course in: as, first of all, my sins I had lived in; and therein I fixed upon this summary of my whole life, that I had made lusts and pleasures my only end, and done nothing with aims at the glory of God; and therefore I would there begin my turning to him, and make the glory of God the measure of all for the time to come.'

This is the account which my dear father drew up concerning the work of the Holy Ghost on his soul, in converting him to God. He left it with a design, as himself said, to give from his own experience a testimony of the difference between common grace, which by some is thought sufficient, and that special saving grace, which indeed is alone sufficient, and always invincibly and effectually prevails, as it did in him, and endured through a long life, and course of various temptations and trials, unto the end. In the first enlightenings and workings of conscience, he experienced how far common grace might go, and yet fail at last, as it did in him, to an utter withering and decay. In the other work on his soul, he felt an extraordinary divine power changing it, and entirely subduing it to God; a work that was lasting and victorious to eternity. I have often heard him say, that in reading the acts of the Synod of Dort, and taking a review of the first workings of common grace in him, he found them consonant with the Arminian opinions; but comparing his own experiences of efficacious grace with the doctrines of the orthodox Protestant divines, he found the one perfectly to agree with the other. It was this inward sense of things, out of which a man will not suffer himself to be disputed, that established him in the truths of the gospel, and possessed him with a due tempered warmth and zeal to assert and vindicate them with such arguments and reasons as the truth is never destitute of to resist gainsayers.

It was many years before he came to have a clear knowledge of the gospel, and a full view of Christ by faith, and to have joy and peace in believing. 'A blessed age this is,' said he in his latter years, 'now the time of faith is come, and faith is principally insisted on unto salvation. In my younger years, we heard little more of Christ than as merely named in the ministry and printed books. I was diverted from Christ for several years, to search only into the signs of grace in me. It was almost seven years ere I was taken off to live by faith on Christ, and God's free love, which are alike the object of faith.' His thoughts for so long a time were chiefly intent on the conviction which God had wrought in him, of the heinousness of sin, and of his own sinful and miserable state by nature ; of the difference between the workings of natural conscience, though enlightened, and the motions of a holy soul, changed and acted by the Spirit, in an effectual work of peculiar saving grace. And accordingly he kept a constant diary, of which I have above a hundred sheets, wrote with his own hand, of observations of the case and posture of his mind and heart toward God, and suitable, pious, and pathetical meditations. His sermons being the result of these, had a great deal of spiritual heat in them, and were blessed by God to the conviction and conversion of many young scholars, who flocked to his ministry : as my reverend brother, Mr Samuel Smith, minister of the gospel at Windsor, told me, that his reverend father, then a young scholar in Cambridge, acknowledged mine to have been blessed by God as an instrument of his conversion, among many others.

As it was that holy minister of Jesus Christ, Mr Price of Lynn, with whom my father maintained a great intimacy of Christian friendship, and of whom he said that he was the greatest man for experimental acquaintance with Christ that ever he met with; and as he poured into his bosom his spiritual complaints, so it was he whose conference by letters and discourse was blessed by God to lead him into the spirit of the gospel, to live by faith in Christ, and to derive from him life and strength for sanctification, and all comfort and joy through believing.

'As for trials of your own heart,' wrote Mr Price to him in one of his letters, 'they are good for you; remember only this, that Christ in whom you believe hath overcome for you, and he will overcome in you : the reason is in 1 John iv. 4. And I say trials are good for you, because else you would not know your own heart, nor that need of continual seeking unto God. But without those trials your spirit would soon grow secure, which of all estates belonging to those that fear God is most dangerous and most uncomfortable. Therefore count it exceeding cause of joy, not of sorrow, when you are exercised with any temptations, because they are tokens of your being in Christ; which being in him Satan would disquiet, and carnal reason would call in question. Yet stand fast in the liberty of Christ, maintain the work of God's free love, which his good Spirit hath wrought in you. Say unto the Lord : Lord, thou knowest I hate my former sinful course; it grieveth me I have been so long such a stranger unto thee, my Father. Thou knowest now I desire to believe in Jesus Christ, I desire to repent of my sins, and it is the desire of my heart to do thy will in all things. Finding these things in your heart, cast yourself upon the righteousness of Christ, and fear nothing; for God will be a most merciful God in Christ unto you. Strive but a little while, and thou shalt be crowned; even so, come, Lord Jesus, come quickly. Amen.'

In another of his letters he thus wrote to him :—

'All your complaints are good, and will bring abundance of thankfulness in the end; for, mark it, in the Scripture, where the saints of God have complained for want of Christ, or any good thing from God in Christ, they have had ere long their hearts and tongues filled with thanksgivings and praise, Rom. vii. 24, 25. It is the surest state for our deceitful hearts to be kept in awe, and not to be as we would be, in perfection of grace. God knows the time when it will be best to fill us with his love, and to ravish us with his favour in Christ. In the meantime let us go on in faith, looking every moment for that day of gladness wherein Christ shall manifest a fuller sight of his blessed presence. I pray you fight it out valiantly by faith in Christ against base unbelief and proud humility. I do assure you, and dare say it, you may by faith in Christ challenge great matters at God's hands, and he will take it well at your hands : yea, the more you can believe for yourself in Christ, the better it will be taken at the throne of grace. Now the Lord give you of his Spirit to help you in all things. The Lord keep your Spirit in Christ, full of faith and love to immortality.'

In another letter he thus wrote :—

'Your last complaint made in your letter of yourself is from spiritual insight of your unregenerate part. It is wholesome, for it being loathed and abhorred, makes Christ in his righteousness and sanctification more glorious in your eyes daily. If this were not, pride and security would start up and undo you. Besides, I find you have great assistance from God in Christ. He ministers much light to you both of knowledge and comfort ; and therefore you had need of some startling evils, to make you depend upon God's grace for the time to come, lest you should rest in that which is past. Let the Lord do what he will with our spirits, so he drive us from the liking ourselves in any sin, and make us long after Christ, to be found in him, and in his righteousness.'

In another he wrote thus :—

'Your letter is welcome to me, and your state also matter of rejoicing unto me, however it may seem unto you for the present. Know you not that the Lord is come to dwell in your heart, and now is purging you and refining you ; that you may be a purer, and also a fitter temple for his Spirit to dwell in? All these things concerning the right framing of your spirit will not be done at once, but by little and little, as it shall please our gracious God in Christ to work for his own glory. Yet this you may have remaining ever unto you, as an evidence of God's everlasting love, that the marks of true chosen ones are imprinted upon you, and truly wrought within you: for your eyes are opened to see yourself utterly lost ; your heart is touched with a sense and feeling of your need of Christ. which is poverty of spirit ; you

hunger and thirst after Christ and his righteousness above all things; and it
is the practice of your inward man to groan and sigh, to ask and seek for
reconciliation with God in Christ. These things you have to comfort you
against sin and Satan, and all the doubts of your own heart. Therefore
when you fear that all is but hypocrisy, to fear is good and wholesome, but
to think so is from the flesh, carnal reason, Satan, darkness, because it is
against that truth which hath taken place in your heart, merely of God's
free favour towards you in Jesus Christ. As for slips and falls, so long as
your purpose is in all things to do the will of God, and to judge yourself for
them, so soon as you find yourself faulty, fear nothing; for these will stick
by you to humble you, and to make you loathe yourself the more, and to
long after the holiness of your blessed Saviour, which is imputed unto you
for your holiness in the sight of God.'

It was thus this gracious minister of Christ, Mr Price, poured the balm of
the gospel into his wounded soul, and God blessed it to heal and comfort it.
These truly evangelical instructions turned his thoughts to Christ, to find
that relief in him which he had in vain sought from all other considerations.
'I am come to this pass now,' wrote my father in a letter to him, 'that signs
will do me no good alone; I have trusted too much to habitual grace for
assurance of justification; I tell you Christ is worth all.' Thus coming
unto Christ, his weary soul found rest, when in all its unquiet motions it
could not find it anywhere else.

But the account of this work of faith I shall give, as I have done the
other, in his own words :—

'It fell out, that soon after my being humbled for sin, the doctrine of justification through Christ by faith came into my thoughts. But my spirit was
turned off from it by this prejudice, that it had been the common deceit
ordinarily of carnal men, when they continued in their sins, and so I might
be deceived in that way and course; and I remembered that I had been
also deceived in believing on Christ crucified with joy and ravishment in my
carnal state; and that remembrance was from time to time a hindrance to
me from going to Christ; and I was pitched on this great principle, that if
I found I were sanctified, as I plainly did, I then was certainly justified.
But I did not think my sanctification to be my justification, but an evidence
of it only; and thus my spirit was set upon examining the inherent work in
me wrought by the Spirit; and I pursued after mortification of lusts, and of
holiness within, and then I thought I should have the comfort of justification,
or of being justified. And thus I was kept from going to Christ actually;
though I dealt with God and his mercy in Christ, as having done all that
was on his part to be done, in redeeming and reconciling us, and so I dealt
immediately with God, and his pure mercy and free grace. But as it fell
strongly into my thoughts, that there was a necessity of Christ's righteousness to justify me, as well as of his grace which had sanctified me; and the
course God took to convince me of it, and to set me a-work about it, was
this. He used the very conviction which I had of original sin from Adam,
in the two branches of it; the guilt of Adam's actual transgression imputed

to me, and the corruption of my nature thence derived. I had had a mighty and large conviction, and deep sense of these, and that all lusts were sins; and this mightily helped me clearly to take in the absolute necessity of justification by Christ's righteousness, and to discern the perfect difference of it from sanctification, and the necessity of it, and I gloried in it. I began to reflect that Jesus Christ was the head for salvation, as Adam had been for sin and condemnation: and that therefore as there were two branches of sin and condemnation derived to me from Adam,—the one an imputation of his fact to me, the other a violent and universal corruption of nature inherent in me,—just so it must be in Christ's salvation of me; and hence I must have an imputation of his righteousness for justification, as well as a holy nature derived from him for sanctification; which righteousness of Christ for justification was perfect, though my sanctification was imperfect. The notion of this did mightily and experimentally enlighten me.'

He now altered his way of preaching, which before had been for the most part, if not wholly, for conviction and terror. But now his experience of the refreshing comforts which the knowledge of Christ, and free justification by his righteousness alone, afforded him, made him zealous to preach the gospel for the consolation of consciences afflicted as his had been. And this was according to the directions given him by that great man, and lively preacher of the gospel, the reverend Dr Sibbs, who by my father's interest among the Fellows had been chosen Master of Catherine Hall, and who familiarly said to him one day, 'Young man, if you ever would do good, you must preach the gospel and the free grace of God in Christ Jesus.' As he called his sermons of the Glory of the Gospel, printed in this fifth volume of his works, his *Primitiæ Evangelicæ*, or his evangelical first-fruits, so the only copy of them was preserved by a remarkable providence. The portmanteau in which they were was by a thief cut off from my father's horse in the dark of the evening, just against St Andrew's Churchyard in Holborn. The clerk or sexton coming on the Lord's-day morning to ring the bell, found a bundle of papers tied up with a string, lying at the foot of a great tree. In it there were some acquittances, which Mr Leonard Green, a bookseller of Cambridge, who had accompanied my father to London, had from some of his customers. It was by these only the clerk could know to whom the bundle did belong, and so he brought it to Mr Green, which he was the more careful to do because he was his particular friend.

He was chosen in 1628 to preach the lecture to the town of Cambridge at Trinity Church. Dr Buckridge, Bishop of Ely, at first made some difficulty of admitting him to it, unless he would solemnly promise, in pursuance of the King's proclamation, not to preach about any controverted points in divinity. My father alleged that the most essential articles of the Christian faith being controverted by one or other, such a promise would scarce leave him any subject to preach on: that it was not his Majesty's intention to inhibit him or any other from preaching against the gross errors of Popery. After some opposition, he was admitted lecturer, and so continued till 1634, when being in his conscience dissatisfied with the terms of conformity, he left the University and his preferments. As he acted herein with all sincerity, following the light which God had given him, and the persuasions of his own mind and conscience, in which no worldly motives had any part,—for if he had hearkened to them, they would have swayed him to a contrary course,—so I have heard him express himself with great joy of faith, and thankfulness and praise of the faithful love of Jesus Christ to him, in performance of that promise, Luke xviii. 29, 30, 'And he said unto them, Verily I say unto you, There is no man that hath left house, or parents, or brethren, or wife, or children, for the kingdom of God's sake, who shall not receive manifold more in this present time, and in the world to come life everlasting.'

'I freely renounced,' said he, 'for Christ, when God converted me, all those designs of pride, and vain-glory, and advancement of myself, upon which my heart was so strongly set that no persuasions of men, nor any worldly considerations, could have diverted me from the pursuit of them. No, it was the power of God alone that prevailed to make me do it. It was he alone made me willing to live in the meanest and most afflicted condition, so that I might serve him in all godly sincerity. I cheerfully parted with all for Christ, and he hath made me abundant compensation, not only in the comforts and joys of his love, which are beyond comparison above all other things, but even in this world. What love and esteem I have had among good men, he gave me. He alone made my ministry in the gospel acceptable, and blessed it with success, to the conversion and spiritual good and comfort of many souls.'

A.D. 1638, he married Mrs Elizabeth Prescott, the daughter of Alderman Prescott: of the other two, one was married to Sir William Leman of Northaw, the other to Sir Nicholas Crisp of Hammersmith. He was very happy in a woman of such a sweet temper, lively wit, and sincere piety, as endeared her to all that knew her. And he was happy in an only daughter he had by her, Elizabeth, who was married to Mr John Mason, a citizen of London. In natural endowments of mind, and, which is far more to be valued, in grace and piety, she was a lively image of her parents. She lost her mother when she was about ten years of age, and died two years before her father's death.

The persecution growing hot in England, my father resolved to remove into some foreign country, where he might exercise his ministry in the gospel, and enjoy the ordinances of Christ according to his conscience, which he could not do in his own native land. He went over into Holland in 1639, settled at last at Arnheim, and was pastor of the English church in that city. During his abode there, some differences arising in the English church at Rotterdam, my father and the elders of the church at Arnheim went thither, and God was pleased to bless their brotherly advice and counsel to compose the differences, and to re-establish the disturbed peace of that church. After some years' continuance in Arnheim, he returned into England, was pastor of a church in London, and by an ordinance of Parliament, June 12, 1643, appointed to be a member of the venerable Assembly of Divines at Westminster. The debates about church government and discipline which arose in that synod are not so proper to be inserted in the life of a particular person. I shall only take notice that he took a brief account of every day's transactions, of which I have fourteen or fifteen volumes in 8vo, wrote with his own hand. And his way of arguing was with such modesty and Christian meekness, that it procured the esteem of those who differed from him and the other dissenting brethren in their judgment.

In the year 1647, he had invitations from the Reverend Mr John Cotton, in whom grace and learning were so happily conjoined, and other worthy ministers in New England, to come over thither, which he was so much inclined to do as he had put a great part of his library on shipboard. But the persuasions of some friends, to whose counsel and advice he paid a great deference, made him to alter his resolution.

In the year 1649, he married Mrs Mary Hammond, descended from the ancient family of the Hammonds in Shropshire, whose ancestor was an officer in the army of William, Duke of Normandy, when he invaded England, A.D. 1066. Though she was but in the seventeenth year of her age, she had the gravity and prudence of a matron. Her conjugal affection, her tender care, her wise administration of the affairs of her family, the goodness of her disposition, and, more than all this, her grace and piety, have left an honourable remembrance of her among all that knew her. He had by her two sons, the eldest of whom is yet living; the other, whose name was Richard, died in a voyage to the East Indies, whither he was sent a year after his father's death by the East India Company, as one of their factors. She also bore to him two daughters, who died in their infancy.

In the same year 1649, he was admitted President of Magdalene College in Oxford, where he made it his business to promote piety and learning. His candour, ingenuous nature, his catholic charity for all good men though of different persuasions, won the hearts of those who had been most averse to him. In conferring any places of preferment at his disposal, he was not biased by affection to a party, but bestowed them where he saw goodness and merit. Those who continued Fellows of the College many years after he left it, Mr Brown, Mr Byfield, and Dr Fairfax, retained an affection and esteem for him, and always spoke of him with an honourable mention. He was not only president of a college, but pastor of a church, which consisted of persons of piety and learning: Mr Thankful Owen, President of St John's; Mr Francis Howell, Master of Jesus College; Mr Theophilus Gale, Mr Stephen Charnock, Mr Blower, Mr Barron, Mr Terry, Mr Lowman, and many others. Upon the Revolution in 1660, he resigned his place of President to Dr Oliver, and removed to London, where he was pastor of the same church which he had gathered in Oxford, a great part of the members of it following him to that city. In the faithful discharge of this office, and labour in the Lord Jesus Christ, he continued till his death.

It was now he lived a retired life, spent in prayer, reading, and meditation, between which he divided his time. He read much, and the authors which he most valued and studied were Augustine, Calvin, Musculus, Zanchius, Paræus, Waleus, Gomarus, Altingius, and Amesius; among the school-men, Suarez

and Estius.   But the Scriptures were what he most studied ; and as he had
furnished his library with a very good collection of commentators, he made
good use of them.   And as the Scriptures are an inexhaustible treasure of
divine knowledge, so by an eager search into them, and comparing one with
another, he discovered those truths which are not to be found in other authors.
The love and free grace of God, the excellencies and glories of our Lord
Jesus Christ, were the truths in which his mind soared with greatest delight.
And it was not merely a speculative pleasure, but these truths were the life
and food of his soul ; and as his heart was affected with them, he wrote
them with a spiritual warmth that is better felt than expressed.   Though
he read much, yet he spent more time in thinking ; and it was by intense
thought that he made himself master of the subject of his discourse.

In that deplorable calamity of the dreadful fire at London, 1666, which
laid in ashes a considerable part of that city, he lost above half his library,
to the value of five hundred pounds.   There was this remarkable, that that
part of it which was lodged very near the place where the fire began, and
which he accounted irrecoverably lost, was by the good providence of God,
and the care and diligence of his very good and faithful friend, Mr Moses
Lowman, though with extreme hazard, preserved from the flames.   But the
other part, which he thought might have been timely secured, being lodged
at as great a distance as Bread Street, was, by the negligence of the person
whom he sent on purpose to take care of them, all burned.   I heard him say
that God had struck him in a very sensible place ; but that as he had loved
his library too well, so God had rebuked him by this affliction.   He blessed
God he had so ordered it in his providence that the loss fell upon those books
which were of human learning ; and that he had preserved those of divinity,
which were chiefly of use to him.   As the exercise of faith, and of patience,
which is the fruit of it, gave him relief, so on this occasion he meditated and
wrote a discourse of ' Patience and its Perfect Work,' printed soon after.

In February 1679, a fever seized him, which in a few days put an end
to his life.   In all the violence of it, he discoursed with that strength
of faith and assurance of Christ's love, with that holy admiration of free
grace, with that joy in believing, and such thanksgivings and praises, as he
extremely moved and affected all that heard him.   That excellent man, Mr
Collins,—who was then pastor of the same church that he had formerly been
pastor of, and with its consent, though unwilling at first to part with him,
he removed to Oxford, 1649, and which is now under the pastoral care of
his worthy son and of Mr Bragg,—praying earnestly for him, offered up this
petition, 'That God would return into his bosom all those comforts which
he had by his ministry of free grace poured into so many distressed souls.'
My dear father felt this prayer answered in the abundant comforts and joys
with which he was filled.   He rejoiced in the thoughts that he was dying,
and going to have a full and uninterrupted communion with God.   'I am
going,' said he, 'to the three Persons, with whom I have had communion :
they have taken me ; I did not take them.   I shall be changed in the twink-
ling of an eye ; all my lusts and corruptions I shall be rid of, which I could

not be here ; those croaking toads will fall off in a moment.' And mentioning those great examples of faith, Heb. xi., 'All these,' said he, 'died in faith. I could not have imagined I should ever have had such a measure of faith in this hour ; no, I could never have imagined it. My bow abides in strength. Is Christ divided ? No, I have the whole of his righteousness ; I am found in him, not in my own righteousness, which is of the law, but in the righteousness which is of God, which is by faith of Jesus Christ, who loved me, and gave himself for me. Christ cannot love me better than he doth ; I think I cannot love Christ better than I do; I am swallowed up in God.'

Directing his speech to his two sons, he exhorted them to value the privilege of the covenant. 'It hath taken hold on me,' said he; 'my mother was a holy woman ; she spake nothing diminishing of it. It is a privilege cannot be valued enough, nor purchased with a great sum of money,' alluding to the words of the chief captain to Paul, Acts xxii. 28. Then he exhorted them to be careful that they did nothing to provoke God to reject them. 'Now,' said he, 'I shall be ever with the Lord.' With this assurance of faith and fulness of joy, his soul left this world, and went to see and enjoy the reality of that blessed state of glory, which in a discourse on that subject he had so well demonstrated. He died February 1679, and in the eightieth year of his age.

HERE LIES THE BODY OF

THE REV. THOMAS GOODWIN, D.D.

BORN AT ROLSEBY,

IN THE COUNTY OF NORFOLK.

HE HAD A LARGE AND FAMILIAR ACQUAINTANCE

WITH ANCIENT,

AND, ABOVE ALL,

WITH ECCLESIASTICAL HISTORY.

HE WAS EXCEEDED BY NONE

IN THE KNOWLEDGE OF THE HOLY SCRIPTURES.

HE WAS AT ONCE BLESSED WITH A RICH INVENTION

AND A SOLID AND EXACT JUDGMENT.

HE CAREFULLY COMPARED TOGETHER

THE DIFFERENT PARTS OF HOLY WRIT;

AND WITH A MARVELLOUS FELICITY

DISCOVERED THE LATENT SENSE

OF THE DIVINE SPIRIT

WHO INDITED THEM.

NONE EVER ENTERED DEEPER

INTO THE MYSTERIES OF THE GOSPEL,

OR MORE CLEARLY UNFOLDED THEM

FOR THE BENEFIT OF OTHERS.

THE MATTER, FORM, DISCIPLINE,

AND ALL THAT RELATES

TO THE CONSTITUTION OF A TRUE CHURCH OF CHRIST,

HE TRACED OUT WITH AN UNCOMMON SAGACITY,

Appendix C: Epitaph on tomb at Bunhill Fields cemetery, London

Continued:

IF HE WAS NOT RATHER THE FIRST DIVINE
WHO THOROUGHLY INVESTIGATED THEM.
HE WAS EMINENTLY QUALIFIED,
BY THE LIGHT OF SACRED TRUTH,
TO PACIFY TROUBLED CONSCIENCES,
TO DISPEL THE CLOUDS OF MISTAKE,
AND REMOVE NEEDLESS SCRUPLES
FROM PERPLEXED AND BEWILDERED MINDS.
IN KNOWLEDGE, WISDOM, AND ELOQUENCE,
HE WAS A TRULY CHRISTIAN PASTOR.
IN HIS PRIVATE DISCOURSES,
AS WELL AS IN HIS PUBLIC MINISTRY,
HE EDIFIED NUMBERS OF SOULS,
WHOM HE HAD FIRST WON TO CHRIST,
TILL HAVING FINISHED HIS APPOINTED COURSE,
BOTH OF SERVICES AND SUFFERINGS
IN THE CAUSE OF HIS DIVINE MASTER,
HE GENTLY FELL ASLEEP IN JESUS,
HIS WRITINGS ALREADY PUBLISHED,
AND WHAT ARE NOW PREPARING FOR PUBLICATION,
THE NOBLEST MONUMENTS OF THIS GREAT MAN'S PRAISE,
WILL DIFFUSE HIS NAME IN A MORE FRAGRANT ODOUR
THAN THAT OF THE RICHEST PERFUME,
TO FLOURISH IN THOSE FAR DISTANT AGES,
WHEN THIS MARBLE, INSCRIBED WITH HIS JUST HONOUR,
SHALL HAVE DROPT INTO DUST.

HE DIED FEBRUARY 23D, 1679,
IN THE EIGHTIETH YEAR OF HIS AGE.

Appendix C: Epitaph on tomb at Bunhill Fields cemetery, London

We who live in the 21st Century, let us thank God for His blessing of having preserved for our benefit, not only His Word, but also the writings of so many God-fearing men who have already gone before us.*

Wherefore seeing we also are compassed about with so great a cloud of witnesses, let us lay aside every weight, and the sin which doth so easily beset us, and let us run with patience the race that is set before us
Hebrews 12:1

* This does not mean in any way, however, that we should venerate, adore, pray to, create a divine image or icon of, or any other such wicked thing, of any of these men, regardless of how God-fearing they may have been. Nor should their writings be treated above, or equal to, God's Word.

For more information about Thomas Goodwin and his other books, please visit our website at:
www.john832publishing.com

Made in the USA
Las Vegas, NV
15 December 2024

14342883R00075